Pilgrimage
Through
the
Watchtower

Pilgrimage Through the Watchtower

Kevin R. Quick

BAKER BOOK HOUSE
Grand Rapids, Michigan 49516

ISBN: 0-8010-7551-3

Contents

"I count all things to be loss in view of the surpassing value of knowing Christ Jesus my Lord, for whom I have suffered the loss of all things, and count them but rubbish in order that I may gain Christ, and may be found in Him, not having a righteousness of my own derived from the Law, but that which is through faith in Christ, the righteousness which comes from God on the basis of faith."

—Philippians 3:8, 9

1

Taking in Knowledge

I was sitting in our living room reading a book by Mahareshi Mahesh Yogi when Steve, my older brother by two years, came in.

"When you're meditating, what are you really doing?" he asked me.

"Well," I said, "according to Mahareshi, when a person meditates, he sets up a special effect in the spirit realm. This attracts the attention of spirit beings living there, and they come to him and help raise his level of consciousness."

"How do you know these aren't demons that you're contacting?" he asked.

"As far as I know, there aren't any such things as demons. When you get to the level of spirit beings, there's nothing evil there. Only good spirits inhabit the spirit realm."

"Well," Steve said, "the Bible says that demons are real. Jesus was continually casting demons out of people. What you believe doesn't agree with the Bible."

He was right, of course. I'd been reading the Bible for about a year by that time, and I could remember reading of many instances where Jesus had cast demons out of people.

"I've stopped meditating," Steve said, "and I think you should too."

Stop meditating! The idea was abhorrent! For the past two years I'd been deeply involved in Eastern teachings, and I had been practicing Transcendental Meditation twice a day for the past year. I was making good progress! To stop meditating now would be ridiculous.

A little later in the day, Steve came to me again. "Come upstairs," he said. "I want to show you something."

I followed him upstairs and we sat on his bed. He opened his Bible and handed it to me. "Read this," he said, "chapter 24. Start at verse 3." I began reading Matthew chapter 24:

> While he was sitting upon the Mount of Olives, the disciples approached him privately, saying: "Tell us, When will these things be, and what will be the sign of your presence and of the conclusion of the system of things?"
> And in answer Jesus said to them: "Look out that nobody misleads you; for many will come on the basis of my name, saying, 'I am the Christ,' and will mislead many. You are going to hear of wars and reports of wars; see that you are not terrified. For these things must take place, but the end is not yet.
> "For nation will rise against nation and kingdom against kingdom, and there will be food shortages and earthquakes in one place after another. All these things are a beginning of pangs of distress" (Matthew 24:3-8, New World Translation).

"How about these signs that Jesus was talking about?" Steve asked. "Wars. Food shortages. Earthquakes. Doesn't this sound like what's happening in the world today? And look what this means. Verse 3 says that these are signs of the 'conclusion of the system of things.' We're living in the last days! The 'conclusion of the system of things' must be really close!"

Now this shook me up a little bit. From my Bible reading

I had come to recognize Jesus as a wonderful teacher. Though I could understand very little of what He said, I found myself both attracted to and terrified by His teachings. He was a different sort of teacher than the others that I had been studying. Jesus' teachings had a power and authority that commanded my deepest respect. And here He was relating 20th-century history in advance, and saying that these things were the signs of the end of this world system!

Steve was learning these things from Jehovah's Witnesses. He had been studying with them for about six months and was now recommending that I do the same. But before I go any further into that story, let me explain first how I got to this point.

I was raised with very little religious background. In my early years I believed that "anything can fill a hole" and that "religion is only for those who need it." I attended church just once while I was growing up, when I was about 12 years old.

In high school I began experimenting with drugs. This led to an intense interest in the supernatural, and I began reading books by such "enlightened" ones as John C. Lilly, Carlos Castaneda, G. I. Gurdjieff, P. D. Ouspensky, and Bagwan Shree Rajneesh. I began experimenting with various mind-control techniques, including Hindu meditations and self-hypnosis.

By the time I entered my freshman year of college I was thoroughly devoted to my quest for "higher consciousness." I enrolled in a Yoga class at the college and began practicing Transcendental Meditation.

About this time I had also begun to read the Scriptures. My grandmother had sent me a New American Standard version of the Bible just after I had entered college. As I began to read it, I found the Bible to be a very intense and mysterious book. It was so hard to understand! Many of the teachings of Jesus seemed to agree with what I was learning in my quest for higher consciousness, yet there were other things that Jesus taught that stood in direct opposition to those teachings. Some of these things made me feel very uneasy, such as Jesus' teachings on eternal judgment and the "weeping and gnashing teeth," the "eternal fire prepared for the Devil and his angels," etc. I was also beginning to see that if the Bible really was the word of God, and Jesus really was who He claimed to be, namely, the Son of God, then truly "there is salvation in no one else; for there is no other name under heaven that has been given among men, by which we must be saved" (Acts 4:12).

So by the time Jehovah's Witnesses arrived on the scene, I was ripe for them. I was reading and trying to understand the Bible on my own, but was having great difficulty. Where else could I turn for help?

There was a Christian in my dorm at college named Don. I met with him several times, hoping that he could help me out. But although he had apparently been a Christian for quite some time, his understanding of the Scriptures was not much better than mine. I remember asking him one day who Matthew was, as I had been reading the gospel of Matthew that week. He had no idea. What was I to do?

By this time my brother Steve had been studying with Jehovah's Witnesses for several months. I couldn't deny that he was learning some wonderful things from them about the Bible, and that I wasn't making the greatest progress on my own. Maybe I should give the JW's a try after all?

I agreed to at least meet with the Witnesses. A week or so later, my brother Steve, my best friend Paul, and I met with Larry and Bob, two of the elders at the local Kingdom Hall of Jehovah's Witnesses in my home town of Hyde Park, New York. I was immediately struck with the Witness elders' command of the Scriptures. Never had I met anyone with such mastery of the Bible! They seemed to have all the answers! I couldn't ask a question but that they would flip through the pages of their Bibles and come up with a Scriptural answer. I was impressed! And since I couldn't deny that the Bible was the Word of God, and that

Jehovah's Witnesses knew a lot more about the Bible than I did, my next step was clear. I would study the Bible with Jehovah's Witnesses.

A few weeks later I drove 260 miles north for my sophomore year at Clarkson University in Potsdam, N.Y. As soon as I arrived I wrote a letter to the local Kingdom Hall asking for someone to study the Bible with me. The following week I received a telephone call from Marshall, the presiding overseer of the Potsdam congregation. He said that he would be happy to study with me, and he mentioned that there was going to be a district convention of Jehovah's Witnesses in Lake Placid that weekend. He invited me to attend, if I could, and he said to look him up if I did come.

I decided to go. I made the 100-mile drive to Lake Placid full of anticipation. What kind of people was I going to find there? Would they all perhaps be the intensely spiritual, God-conscious people that I had been looking for in my search for Truth?

I arrived at the convention center and was met at the door by a gentleman in a three-piece suit who handed me a copy of the convention program. I walked inside and was, to my dismay, thoroughly let down. The convention looked like a huge business meeting of some sort. Everyone was dressed in very businesslike fashion. About 2,000 people were sitting quietly in their seats listening to an older gentleman on the platform lecturing on various organizational instructions. I listened to the talk for a few minutes and gazed around at the people sitting in their seats. They looked like just regular, ordinary people. I walked out into the hallway and strolled around for awhile. If these were God's people, I thought to myself, I was going to have a hard time adjusting to this!

I was supposed to look for Marshall, but I had lost all desire to do so. I left after having been at the convention less than 10 minutes, and drove back to Potsdam. Though I was to study with Marshall for the next three years and become very close to him, I never had the heart to tell him that I had been at the convention.

Marshall and his wife, Meryl, were wonderful people. During my last three years of college they became my second family. Every week either Marshall would come to my dorm room or I would go to his house for a Bible Study. I often had dinner with them at their home, and we became very close. Marshall was the custodian at the high school in Potsdam, and lived in a small mobile home out in the country with Meryl and their two children. Potsdam winters were very cold, and the warmth and love that I found in their home was wonderful. My Bible studies with Marshall and fellowship with his family were also great ways to escape the pressures of college life and the coldness of my technical studies. But best of all, I was learning from Marshall and Meryl many things about my Creator, Jehovah God.

During the summers, when I was at home in Hyde Park, I studied with Larry, one of the two elders that I had met with previously at the Kingdom Hall, and Dotti, his wife. I studied with them at their home for several hours each week. At one of these studies, Dotti, a full-time "pioneer," said something that really stuck in my heart. She told me that if she ever found out that Jehovah's Witnesses did not have the Truth, she would leave. She was a servant of God, not men.

Also during the summers, my brother Steve and I would often drive across the Hudson River to Watchtower Farms, a 45-minute drive, to hear special talks at the Kingdom Hall there. Zone overseers, missionaries from distant lands, and even members of the Governing Body (the 13- to 17-member body which governs all the affairs of Jehovah's Witnesses) would give these talks. What a privilege! My favorite talk was one given by Raymond Franz, who was at the time a member of the Governing Body. He spoke in depth about the first-century Corinthian congregation: its people, cultural background, the conditions prompting Paul's letters, etc. I recorded this talk on cassette tape and listened to it many times in my car on my way to and from my summer job at IBM in Poughkeepsie. One thing that he said in the talk really made a strong impression on me. He said that when encouraging his brothers, it is better for a Christian to give simple, heartfelt expressions of his faith than to make great displays of Bible knowledge. A few years later I was heartbroken to hear that Ray had been disfellowshipped (excommunicated) for "apostasy."

During these three and a half years that I studied with Jehovah's Witnesses, I spent an average of two hours per day reading the Bible and assorted Watchtower Society publications. While at college, I would often spend five or six hours at a time at the Potsdam State University library studying these books. By the time I was baptized in the spring of 1981, I had read over 30 of the Society's books and all of the *Watchtower* and *Awake!* magazines for those years, and I had read the New World Translation of the Bible through several times.

In the spring of 1980 I graduated from Clarkson with a bachelor of science degree in mechanical engineering. By this time I had adopted the Society's view of higher education and decided not to attend my "worldly" graduation ceremony. In fact, during my last couple of years of college, and for several years thereafter, I found myself almost apologizing to my Witness friends for having even gone to college. A college graduate amongst Jehovah's Witnesses is generally viewed with suspicion. His "worldly wisdom" makes it difficult for him to remain humble and submissive to the "mother" organization.

After graduation, I packed up and moved to Colorado Springs, Colorado. Digital Equipment Corporation had flown me out to Colorado Springs for an interview. Although Digital did not make me a job offer, I loved Colorado and decided to move out there anyway. There were many new computer and electronics companies moving into Colorado Springs, and I figured that I'd find an engineering job there without too much trouble.

But there were much stronger reasons for my moving to Colorado. Life at home was becoming unbearable. By this time I had stopped celebrating my birthday, Christmas and all the other "pagan" holidays. I had made known my stand on the blood transfusion issue (Jehovah's Witnesses will not accept blood transfusions, even in life-threatening situations). As a result, my mother was becoming extremely frustrated with me and was often moved to tears when trying to reason with me. But since she had very little knowledge of the Bible and was wholly without Scriptural support for her arguments, I was determined to serve God rather than men.

My father was no more kindly disposed toward the Witnesses than was my mom. I later found out that when Jehovah's Witnesses were planning to build the Kingdom Hall at the end of our residential street, my father had formed a committee to try to keep the Witnesses out of the neighborhood. Not only had his efforts to stop them from building the Kingdom Hall failed, but now two of his sons were walking down to the new Kingdom Hall three times a week to attend their meetings!

One day a couple of sisters out in "field service" came to our door. After giving them a thorough chewing out for tearing his family apart, my father went down into the basement, found a can of spray paint, and called Steve to the front door. "You tell those girls," he said, "that if they ever come back here again, I'm not going to say a word to them, but'll just spray them with this paint," and he put the can next to the door. The paint was never used, as far as I know.

My best friend Paul wasn't helping things much, either. He had gotten ahold of the book, *Thirty Years a Watchtower Slave* by William Schnell, and had given it to my mom. She read it, and in tears, pleaded with me to read it too. I read about half of the book and gave it back to Paul. It looked to me as though Mr. Schnell simply had a grudge against the Society and this book was his way of venting his anger. It did little for me.

At this time I was convinced that the persecution that I was experiencing at home was a sure sign that I was coming into "God's organization." "A man's enemies will be the members of his household (Matt 10:36)." But then, in all of this, not once was I persecuted for the name of Jesus. This would come a few years later.

Before moving to Colorado Springs, I prayed to Jehovah that He would direct me to the proper congregation. There were thirteen congregations of Jehovah's Witnesses in Colorado Springs. I was confident that He would direct my steps.

I ended up at the Foothills congregation of Jehovah's Witnesses in Manitou Springs. To my disappointment, the first meeting that I attended, a Sunday morning public talk and Watchtower study, brought back all of the disappointing memories of that first district convention in Lake Placid. The meeting was awful! The public talk, given by one of the congregation's elders, was terribly boring, and the Watchtower study was even worse. A paragraph or two of the week's study article was read in a monotone by a brother on the platform, the Watchtower study conductor read the question at the bottom of the page, and the congregation offered robot-like answers from sentences that they had underlined in their magazines. What kind of meeting was this? From my association with many of the "Farm brothers" in New York, I had become accustomed to hearing answers given from the heart by brothers who really wanted to contribute something to the meeting. But this meeting was nothing like that. Could this congregation really be where Jehovah wanted me? I even contemplated writing a letter to the Society to let them know that this congregation needed help. But then, no, maybe Jehovah had arranged this whole thing after all. Maybe I was here to help stir things up. Maybe Jehovah had planted me here as a source of encouragement to my brothers. Let God's will be done, I acquiesced.

The first month of Foothills meetings that I attended I spent looking for someone who might enjoy studying with me, and I with him. There was in the Foothills congregation a young ex-Bethelite (one who had worked at Bethel, the world headquarters of Jehovah's Witnesses in

Brooklyn, N.Y.) named Dean, who seemed to be the most likely candidate. I approached Dean one evening after the weekly Service meeting and asked if he would like to study with me. He readily agreed, and we soon became the closest of friends.

I studied with Dean for a year. Then, on an off-road motorcycle ride in the Colorado Rockies on a beautiful spring day in 1981, after three and a half years of diligent study, meditation, and intensive prayer, I dedicated my life to Jehovah God. That evening I informed Dean of my desire to be baptized. Shortly thereafter, on three separate occasions, I met with the Foothills elders, who reviewed with me the "80 questions for baptismal candidates" in the *Organized to Accomplish Our Ministry* book. Then, at the 1981 "Kingdom Loyalty" district convention of Jehovah's Witnesses in Denver, I was baptized. I was now, at last, a full-fledged, baptized Witness of Jehovah!

2

What Jehovah's Witnesses Believe

Before getting into the doctrinal teachings of Jehovah's Witnesses, I think I should say something first about Watchtower hermeneutics, study methods, and Bible translations.

Watchtower Hermeneutics

Asking a Jehovah's Witness about Biblical hermeneutics is almost guaranteed to draw a blank from the Witness. "Hermeneutics" (the science of Biblical interpretation) is a foreign word to most Witnesses. Because the Watchtower Society is "God's Organization," they reason, all Bible interpretation that it supplies is therefore correct, being directed by God Himself. They therefore see no need for their own personal understanding of hermeneutics.

When one begins to explore Watchtower theology from an objective (non-Witness) viewpoint, he quickly discovers that the established, consistent rules of Biblical hermeneutics have been discarded by the Society in favor of "rules" that enable Watchtower expositors to force Scripture verses to fit the current Watchtower mold. This can be seen in both the

Watchtower's re-formulation of basic Christian doctrine as well as in its interpretation of prophecy. With doctrine, the Witness expositors recognize that "on the surface" many Bible verses clearly contradict the teachings of the Society. These verses are therefore "spiritualized" and often interpreted to mean precisely the opposite of what they actually say! With prophecy, this "spiritualized" method enables Watchtower theologians to wrest the application of Biblical prophecies from the people to whom they were originally given (the nation Israel, for example) in order to apply them to "Jehovah's modern-day organization."

Frequent use of this allegorical or "spiritualized" method of interpretation also creates another convenient situation for the Society. If much of Scripture is to be applied "spiritually," or "symbolically," then how are we to know how to interpret the Bible at all? How are we to know which passages are to be understood "spiritually" and which are to be taken literally? Hence arises the need for a special class of Bible interpreters, the "faithful and discreet slave class." The average Witness himself is very careful not to accept the Bible's teachings at face value. He will instead look to the "slave class" to provide all necessary interpretation for him.

We will consider a much more consistent and satisfactory method of Biblical interpretation, the grammatico-historical method, in chapter six.

Study Methods

The Watchtower has only one recognized Bible study method. Actually, it's probably stretching things to call it a Bible study method at all. It would be more accurate to call it "book study," "indoctrination," or even "brainwashing." Whether it's the Watchtower study on Sunday morning, the book study on Tuesday evening, or a "Bible study" with an interested person in his home, the study method is always the same. A "reader" reads aloud a paragraph or two from the Watchtower publication being studied. The "study conductor" reads the corresponding question that's printed at the bottom of the page. The students then answer the question, usually by reading what they have underlined in their own copies of the study material. Scripture texts are looked up and read to confirm the answers given in the paragraph. This procedure is followed paragraph by paragraph until the entire Watchtower article or the chapter in the book is covered. Some individual comments are encouraged, but no deviation from the basic "study" method is allowed.

This process is repeated article by article, day after day, week after week, year after year. The Society's viewpoints, via the Watchtower's voluminous study material, is rehashed again and again. As a result every Jehovah's Witness, regardless of his educational background, is able to parrot the Society's views on virtually any subject. Independent analytical thinking is eventually discarded altogether, and the Witness "discipleship" is then complete. He has completely "made his mind over."

I often wondered why we used these methods in our studies. "If this is the Truth," I wondered, "why virtually brainwash ourselves like this? Why not have open discussions and challenge one another in our studies? Why repeat the same presentations, the same studies on the same topics again and again?" I reasoned that since most Jehovah's Witnesses were not very well educated, this must be the only way that they could learn. Besides, which was more important, the Truth or the manner in which the Truth was presented? God had simply given us our "food at the proper time" in such a way that all of His people could easily digest it.

Especially at the beginning, I had a lot of questions, and I usually asked them at the meetings. I was very careful how I worded my questions, however, trying not to appear as one who might be critical of the organization. Honest questions from a new prospect like me were tolerated somewhat, as long as they didn't disrupt the flow of the meeting. But as I was to find out soon enough, questioning by a dedicated, baptized Witness, even on the smallest point of doctrine, would not be tolerated and could very likely be grounds for disfellowshipping!

Individual Bible study groups not sanctioned by Watchtower headquarters in Brooklyn are strictly forbidden amongst Jehovah's Witnesses. I was to find this out first-hand. We had a group of young people in Manitou Springs who got together to study the Watchtower and to encourage one another every Monday evening. After our group had been meeting for several weeks, the elders of our congregation, after discussing the situation with our circuit overseer,[1] disbanded it. We were told that our get-togethers were outside of Watchtower Society regulations. And this, even though we were only studying the Watchtower! Independent study and discussion of the Bible without "mother's" direct supervision is strictly forbidden amongst Jehovah's Witnesses.

Bible Translations

Jehovah's Witnesses rarely use any Bible translation other than their own "New World Translation." All other translations are viewed with suspicion, being the products of supposedly "biased" Trinitarian scholars. It is felt amongst the Witnesses that since the standard, reputable translations were produced by scholars who believed in the Trinity, their translations were therefore "slanted" or mistranslated to support their own views of the Godhead. The same "slanting" was supposedly used by these translators to uphold all other historic Christian doctrines as well, including the nature of the soul, the nature of hell, etc. The standard translations, therefore, are not trusted by Jehovah's Witnesses. Isolated texts, however, are sometimes quoted from translations other than the NWT if they seem to support Witness viewpoints. Psalm 83:18, for example, is often quoted from the King James version since the tetragrammaton (Heb. YHWH, usually translated "LORD" or "Jehovah") is there translated "Jehovah." Witnesses often use this verse to show their prospective converts God's Name in their own Bibles.

In contrast with the "Trinitarian" translations, the Watchtower Society hails its own New World Translation as the most unbiased and accurate translation available today.[2] The *New World Translation of the Christian Greek Scriptures,* produced by the New World Translation Committee, first appeared in 1950. The *New World Translation of the Hebrew-Aramaic Scriptures* was soon thereafter released in five volumes, the first volume being completed in 1953 and the final volume in 1960. Today the complete New World Translation is published in one volume.

The members of the New World Translation Committee, all of whom were Jehovah's Witnesses, have remained anonymous. They have supposedly assumed this position out of humility, preferring that all credit for the translation go to God alone. Conveniently, though, the anonymity of the Committee members has made any investigation into their scholastic credentials virtually impossible. However, insights into the identities and qualifications of the members of the NWT Translation committee have been offered by a former member of the Brooklyn headquarters staff.[3]

We'll reserve a technical discussion of the New World Translation for chapter six.

Doctrines of Jehovah's Witnesses

Just what do Jehovah's Witnesses believe? The following is a brief overview of their teachings.

God

Jehovah is the only true God.[4] Jesus is "a" god, a "mighty" god, but not Almighty God.[5] Holy spirit is God's "active force" and is devoid of personality.[6] There is no plurality in the Godhead.[7] The doctrine of the Trinity is of pagan origin.[8]

Jehovah God, the Father, first created Jesus, then all other things were created through Jesus.[9] It is not proper to pray to Jesus.[10] Prayer is to be directed to the Father alone, *through* Jesus.[11] It is not proper to worship Jesus.[12] Worship belongs to the Father alone.[13]

Man

The composition of man can be summed up by the formula "body + spirit = soul."[14] It is incorrect to say that man has a soul; rather, man *is* a soul.[15] There is no soul that lives on after the death of the body.[16] Man's spirit also has no existence apart from the body.[17] At death the spirit dissipates.[18] There is no conscious afterlife.[19] God retains only the memory of the one who has died.[20]

Jesus was not raised with a physical body.[21] Likewise, the bodies of Christians with the "heavenly hope" will not be resurrected.[22] They, like Jesus, will be re-created as spirits.[23]

Hell, as the term is commonly understood, does not exist.[24] It is impossible for one to experience either blessing or torment in Hades.[25] Those cast into gehenna or the lake of fire go off into eternal nonexistence.[26]

God's People

The nation Israel was at one time God's chosen people, but was cast off forever in 70 C.E.[27] Unfulfilled prophecy given to natural Israel is to have fulfillment in "spiritual Israel," the Christian congregation.[28] Jehovah's kingdom program does not include the restoration of natural Israel.[29]

The "little flock" of Luke 12:32 is equated with the 144,000 of Revelation chapters 7 and 14.[30] The 144,000 are sealed from among all nations to become "spiritual Israel."[31] The sealing of the 144,000 began at Pentecost, 33 C.E., and continues to the present day.[32] The 144,000 are sealed to be kings, priests, and the bride of Christ.[33] Only these 144,000 Christians will go to heaven to be with Christ.[34]

The "faithful and discreet slave" of Matthew 24:45 represents the "anointed remnant" of Jehovah's Witnesses which has been responsible for overseeing the kingdom-preaching work in modern times.[35] The "faithful and discreet slave class" was identified and rewarded shortly after Christ's invisible return in the year 1914.[36] The "slave class" is now in charge of all of Christ's earthly belongings.[37] Acquiring the "accurate knowledge" dispensed by this "slave class" is essential to a Christian's salvation.[38] In order to receive divine approval on his life, a Christian must willingly submit to all the teachings of the "slave class."[39]

The "other sheep" of John 10:16 are equated with the "great crowd" of Revelation 7:9.[40] This group presently comprises 99.7% of Jehovah's Witnesses.[41] Members of the "great crowd" are not to be born again.[42] They will pass through the imminent great tribulation and will enter directly into everlasting life on earth.[43]

The so-called Christian church, or Christendom, is identified with the harlot, "Babylon the Great" of Revelation chapters 17 and 18.[44] She is hopelessly apostate and will soon be completely destroyed by Jehovah.[45] In these last days God is dealing exclusively with the Watchtower Bible and Tract Society and with those who are responding favorably to its teachings.[46] One can only come to understand the Bible and God's purposes by associating with this earthly organization.[47] One's salvation is dependent upon his favorable response to the teachings of this organization.[48]

Salvation

The gospel to be preached now is primarily the good news that the kingdom of God was invisibly established in the year 1914.[49] By believing in Christ and by taking refuge in Jehovah's organization, men can now hope to survive the great tribulation and enter directly into the earthly realm of the kingdom.[50] This "gospel" is in complete harmony with that preached by Paul and the other early disciples.[51]

To be "born again" means to be begotten by holy spirit so

as to have hope of a heavenly resurrection.[52] Only 144,000 Christians are to be born again, of whom approximately 9,000 are presently alive on earth.[53] The other 3,000,000+ present-day Jehovah's Witnesses have an "earthly hope" and have no need of being born again.[54]

It is improper for a Christian to say that he "is saved."[55] He has no assurance of salvation.[56] He awaits future salvation.[57]

To be saved a person must take in knowledge,[58] believe in Jesus Christ,[59] repent,[60] dedicate himself to Jehovah,[61] turn around,[62] recognize the Watchtower Society as "God's organization,"[63] conduct his life in harmony with the teachings and activities of the Watchtower Society,[64] maintain integrity to Jehovah and to his earthly organization,[65] and endure faithfully to the end.[66] The redemptive work of Christ alone is not sufficient for the justification of a believer.[67]

A Christian must not come directly to Jesus for salvation, but only to the Father (Jehovah) *through* Jesus.[68] Only the members of the 144,000 are under the new covenant by virtue of Christ's blood and may rightly partake of the bread and wine at the Memorial (Communion).[69] The "other sheep" are to be merely observers at the Memorial.[70]

The Last Days

The duration of the "Gentile Times" can be ascertained to be 2,520 years by a study of Daniel chapter 4.[71] They began in 607 B.C.E. with the onset of Israel's Babylonian captivity and ended in the fall of 1914 C.E. with the invisible return of Christ.[72] The signs of Christ's return began after his return in 1914 and give evidence that he is now invisibly present.[73] Christ will not have a visible return to earth.[74]

The "rapture" occurred invisibly in the year 1918.[75] The bodily translation of the Christian church is a false hope and will not occur.[76]

Christ will not be physically present on earth during the

millennium.[77] The 144,000 of Revelation chapters 7 and 14 will rule invisibly with Christ during the millennium.[78] The "great crowd" of Revelation chapter 7 will live through the great tribulation and will enter directly into the cleansed earth.[79] They will inhabit the earth during the millennium.[80] This "earthly hope" is the Biblical hope for the majority of true Christians alive today.[81]

The present heaven and the present earth will be cleansed and will remain forever.[82] A new heaven and earth will not be created.[83]

Summary

As can be seen from this brief synopsis of Watchtower doctrine, the primary thrust of Jehovah's Witnesses' teachings and evangelistic efforts is to discredit and if possible, to completely destroy the age-old tenets of historic Christianity. The foundational doctrines of historic Christianity, including the deity and bodily resurrection of Christ, the personality of the Holy Spirit, the triune nature of God, salvation by grace, the rapture of the Church, and the visible return of Christ are all vehemently denied by Jehovah's Witnesses. Are the individual Witnesses themselves perhaps ignorant of this fact? By no means! Rather, they rejoice in it! How wonderful to be members of "God's organization," so boldly tearing down Christendom's hoary "doctrines of demons" and replacing them with "the truth of God's word"! Indeed, how wonderful to be Jehovah's instruments in executing such a lofty, divine purpose!

To accomplish this "divine purpose," the Watchtower Society has developed an intensive program of indoctrination and ministerial preparation for its members, as well as a massive evangelistic campaign to bring its "life saving" message to the ends of the earth. How this program is carried out, the nuts and bolts of it, is the subject of our next chapter.

3

Life in the "New World Society"

Life as a Witness is by no means an easy one. Many long, self-sacrificing hours are spent each week in personal study, preparing for and attending meetings, delivering public talks at the Kingdom Hall, engaging in "field service," and studying with interested persons in their homes. In addition, circuit assemblies and district conventions are prepared for and attended three times each year.

Meetings

Jehovah's Witnesses attend five meetings each week: the public talk, the Watchtower study, the book study, the Theocratic Ministry School, and the Service Meeting.

The public talk is usually given on Sunday morning. It's given by one of the local congregation elders, or possibly by a visiting elder from a nearby congregation. If the circuit overseer is in town, he'll give the public talk.

The public talk is forty-five minutes long and is taken from an outline provided by the Watchtower Society. The talk usually revolves around a particular theme such as world conditions, Bible prophecy, or Christian conduct.

The public talk is, as is every meeting, preceded and followed by congregational prayer and a "kingdom song" (I

27

often played the piano accompaniment in Manitou Springs).

The public talk is followed immediately by the Watchtower study. At the Watchtower study, a "reader" reads the prescribed study article from the Watchtower magazine, paragraph by paragraph, the Watchtower study conductor asks the questions at the bottoms of the pages of the magazine, and the congregation members answer the questions. The Watchtower study articles are the main source of "spiritual food" for Jehovah's Witnesses. The weekly study article is usually relevant to a current subject or need in the organization, such as the exposition of Watchtower doctrine, application of Bible prophecy to current events, discussion of moral issues, etc. The study takes about an hour.

The book study, conducted in small groups in private homes, can be held at any time during the week, but is usually held on a Tuesday, Wednesday, or Thursday evening. The book study follows the same format as the Sunday morning Watchtower study, except that the study may be conducted by either a congregation elder or a ministerial servant (the Watchtower counterpart of the Christian deacon), and the subject material is taken from an assigned book rather than the Watchtower magazine. The book study takes an hour.

The Theocratic Ministry School meeting is conducted on a weeknight other than that of the book study, usually Thursday or Friday evening, and is held at the Kingdom Hall. At this meeting there is a series of five talks: the instruction talk, the Bible reading or #2 talk, the #3 talk, the #4 talk, and the #5 talk. The instruction talk is a fifteen-minute lecture given by one of the congregation elders or ministerial servants. The Bible reading is just that, a reading of a chapter or so from the New World Translation, usually done by a younger or newer member of the Ministry School. The #3 and #4 talks are each five minutes long and are usually discussions by two "sisters." The #5 talk is a five-minute talk based on a recent Watchtower or

"Awake!" article, usually given by a moderately experienced speaker. After each of these talks a public critique of the student's presentation is given by the Ministry School overseer. Suggestions are given on areas that may need work including timing (timing seems to be of particular importance; the Ministry School overseer times each talk with a stopwatch), voice inflection, gestures, etc. The entire Ministry School meeting takes about an hour.

Once every three months the Theocratic Ministry School is preempted by the "written review." The written review is a written true-or-false, fill-in-the-blank, and multiple-choice test covering the material studied in the Ministry School over the past several months. After the congregation has had 45 minutes or so to complete the review, the correct answers to the questions are given from the platform. Each student grades his own paper. No records are kept on the test scores.

As with virtually everything else in Witness life, personal testimony and expression have very little place in the Theocratic Ministry School. A personal example will illustrate this point.

As a relatively new student in the Ministry School at the Foothills congregation in Manitou Springs, Colorado, I was assigned a #5 talk. The "Awake!" article that I was to base my talk on was entitled, "Do All Religions Lead to God?" I made the mistake of incorporating some of my personal background, how I was involved with Eastern teachings before coming into "the Truth," into my introduction. Though the congregation noticeably enjoyed my talk, one of the congregation elders pulled me aside after the meeting and "counseled" me on my introduction. He felt that relating my own personal experiences to the congregation was inappropriate. After this I was careful not to include such elements in my talks.

The Service Meeting follows immediately after the Theocratic Ministry School meeting. This meeting is to prepare the congregation members for their door-to-door "field service" activity. The Service Meeting has all the trappings of a corporate sales meeting. Articles in the monthly "Our Kingdom Ministry" newsletter are reviewed by the congregation to inculcate various witnessing methods, together with literature sales and distribution techniques. Special offers for the month are discussed. Sample presentations are given. Statistics as to the numbers of books and magazines sold, the numbers of hours spent in door-to-door activity and home Bible studies, and the number of new converts baptized are reviewed. Encouragement is given for all to participate in the field ministry on the coming weekend and during the following week.

"Field Service"

Door-to-door evangelism is not an elective for Jehovah's Witnesses. It's an obligation. The average Witness's reasoning on this is usually something like the following:

Matthew 24:14 (NWT) states, "And this good news of the kingdom will be preached in all the inhabited earth for a witness to all the nations; and then the end will come." First John 2:17 says, "the world is passing away and so is its desire, but he that does the will of God remains forever." Jehovah's Witnesses believe that they are fulfilling Matthew 24:14 by preaching their version of the "good news of the kingdom." This preaching is therefore the present-day will of God. Coupling this with 1 John 2:17, then, those who do not take part in the preaching work will pass away with the rest of the world at Armageddon. If a Witness hopes to survive Armageddon, he must preach. This is further "confirmed" by Ezekiel 3:18, where Jehovah says to Ezekiel, "When I say to someone wicked, 'You will positively die,' and you do not actually warn him and speak in order to warn the wicked one from his wicked way to preserve him alive, he being wicked, in this error he will die, but his blood I shall ask back from your own hand."

Each "field service" session is preceded by a 15-minute "meeting for service," held either at the Kingdom Hall or at a private home. At this meeting, the "daily text" (a verse or two of Scripture with a short Watchtower Society comment from the current Yearbook) is discussed, "territory cards" (each congregation's "territory" is subdivided and printed on 3" x 5" "territory cards") are checked out, and logistical arrangements are made for the day's activities. Those present then divide into "car groups" and drive to their respective "territories."

On arriving at the territory, the car group divides into pairs of Witnesses for the door-to-door activity. Sometimes an experienced Witness will pair up with a less experienced Witness for training purposes, but this is not always the case. Family, relatives, and close friends will often pair up for the sake of comraderie. After the car group has paired off, the Witnesses, Bibles and Watchtower literature in hand, commence their "preaching" and "disciple-making work."

Each home or apartment is approached, and the "householder" is greeted and engaged in conversation, usually regarding present world conditions or some other topic of general interest. At some point in the conversation, God's millennial kingdom is presented by the Witness as the solution to the problem being discussed. To help the householder in learning more about Jehovah and his kingdom, an offer is made for the purchase of the Watchtower and Awake! magazines. If the householder purchases the literature or in some other way shows interest, arrangements are made for a "return visit" the following week. These "return visits" continue as long as the householder continues to show interest. Eventually, the householder is encouraged to accept a "free home Bible study." If he accepts, the Witness returns once each week to study a current Watchtower Society publication with him, one chapter per week. At the time of this writing, the book *You Can Live Forever in Paradise on Earth* is being used for this purpose. After a few weeks of study, when the time is right, the Witness asks the "interested person" if he would like to attend one of their meetings at the Kingdom Hall. The interested person often accepts the invitation, is soon attending all five meetings each week, and is encouraged to enroll in the "Theocratic Ministry School." Then, if he has been progressing well in his studies, he is prodded by his many new Witness friends to get baptized. He finally concedes, makes a personal commitment to Jehovah, and becomes a "baptismal candidate." He then meets with the elders of his congregation on three separate occasions to review the "80 questions for baptismal candidates" in the *Organized to Accomplish Our Ministry* book. Upon completion of these sessions, he is eligible for baptism. The baptism itself takes place either at a local private pool, or more often at an upcoming circuit or district convention of Jehovah's Witnesses. Now baptized, the convert has completed his induction into the Watchtower society: from "householder" to "return visit" to "interested person" to "Bible study" to "baptismal candidate" to one of Jehovah's dedicated, baptized Witnesses!

A typical Witness puts in an average of seven to eight hours of "field service" per month. I personally put in from five to six hours per month, a little less than the national (U.S.) average. During the three and a half years that I spent as a bona fide, baptized Witness, however, I was never "irregular" in field service. I never let a month go by without sharing in the witnessing work.

Field service was at first terrifying and humiliating for me, but later on was often enjoyable. I personally loved the Bible, and thoroughly enjoyed any opportunities that I had to discuss it with others, rare as they might be. The vast majority of people, whether professedly Christian or not, were simply "not interested." A few misguided Christian people did "God bless" us and encourage us in our witnessing activity, though they still refused to discuss the Scriptures with us. I'm sure that if they had known our real purpose in calling, namely, to replace their orthodox Christian faith with the "good news of Jehovah's established (since 1914) kingdom," they would have been a bit more reserved in bestowing their blessings upon us (Gal 1:8, 9)!

Others that we met were more hostile. One day, for example, working in the Crystal Hills area of Manitou Springs with Dean, a middle-aged man, a retired army colonel, came to the door. He had an angry expression on his face and a large pair of scissors in his hand. "Are you Jehovah's Witnesses?" he asked me (it was "my door"). I answered, "Yes, we are." He said, "I have two questions for you. Will you salute the flag of the United States of America?" I answered, "No." He asked, "Will you bear arms and fight for your country?" I said, "No, but I'd like to explain . . ." He cut me off and sneered, "You have thirty seconds to get off my property!" Dean and I made haste back out to the street and continued on our way.

With all the apathy amongst the people in general, and with so much blind hatred and antagonism from others, you'd think that I'd remember at least one instance where I was greeted by a loving Christian who was eager to witness to me (share his testimony, debate the Scriptures, or whatever), but sadly, such was not the case. Christians, please hear me. *In the seven years that I spent going from door to door with a Bible in my hand, preaching what I believed to be the gospel, not once did a concerned Christian invite me in or even come outside* (if 2 John 10 bothered him) *to discuss the Scriptures with me.* Looking back, the most "Christian" response that I can remember occurred while I was studying with the Witnesses in Potsdam, New York. Jim, a newly baptized Witness, and I were going from house to house. We approached one home where an older woman came to the door and asked, "Are you Jehovah's Witnesses?" We answered, "Yes." She said, "Oh, please come in!" so we did. "John," she said to her husband as she ushered us into the kitchen, "I think we should pray for these boys." Then she and her husband bowed their heads and began praying for us! But to our Watchtower minds, these "Babylonian religionists" were praying to their three-headed deity, and were probably calling demons down upon us! We had to get out of there fast! Leaving the woman and her husband in the kitchen praying, Jim and I made a dash across the living room and escaped out the front door.

Jehovah's Witnesses keep meticulous records of their door-to-door activities. "Time reports" are filled out every month by each active Witness. These reports detail the number of hours spent in field service each month, the numbers of books and magazines sold, and the number of "Bible studies" conducted. These reports are reviewed by the congregation elders and a "publisher's card," a sort of permanent report card, is kept on the "publisher," or individual Witness. The circuit overseer examines these publisher's cards and all other congregation records during his thrice-yearly visits. The publisher card follows the Witness wherever he goes. When I moved from Colorado back to New York in 1983, for example, my publisher card was sent also. The elders of my new congregation were then able to immediately judge my past door-to-door performance and to counsel me accordingly.

For me, as for the typical Witness, filling out the time report was a very unpleasant monthly ritual (Dotti, the "pioneer" sister and wife of the elder in Hyde Park who studied with me, once told me that she also hated it). Filling out the report always made me feel so guilty. I knew that I could have put in a few more hours that month if I had only tried a little harder. Though I evidently enjoyed reading and studying the Bible more than most Witnesses, the real praise and acclamation went to those who served sacrificially in the door-to-door work. The "pioneers" (who put in 90 hours of witnessing activity per month) and the "auxiliary pioneers" (60 hours per month) were routinely called up to the platform to be applauded by the rest of the congregation. I remember during one of these episodes turning to Dean, who was sitting next to me, and saying, "I feel like getting up and saying, 'Now let's hear it for the rest of us schlepps!'"

Another example will serve to show the importance placed upon field service hours. For several months I served regularly as a "reader" for the Watchtower study in

Manitou Springs. Quite a few members of the congregation let me know that they enjoyed my reading, and I personally enjoyed serving Jehovah in this small way. Then the elders of the congregation made a ruling that only those who consistently put in at least ten hours of "time" per month would be allowed to do the public reading. I was told that I could no longer do the reading until my "hours" were "brought up," and I was taken off the reading schedule.

The time-counting system bothered me also in several other ways. For one, I knew of several Witnesses, even some pioneers, who routinely "padded" their time in order to make their 60-hour or 90-hour quotas. "I'll make up the difference next month," they'd say. Also, there was a group in Manitou Springs who would "meet for service" at 9:00 a.m., get to the "field" at 9:30, go door-to-door for 45 minutes, and at 10:30 sharp congregate at the Manitou Coffee Shop for breakfast. Then they'd return to the "field" at 11:30 for a final half hour of Witnessing. This was reckoned by many of them as three hours of field service. From these and many other experiences I came to realize that not all Witnesses are genuinely interested in speaking to people about Jehovah. Not a few of them are simply "putting in time."

Assemblies

In addition to their five meetings per week, Jehovah's Witnesses also attend circuit assemblies twice each year and district conventions once each year.

Circuit assemblies are generally held in large auditoriums capable of seating from two to ten thousand people, and are attended by the twenty or so congregations that make up that particular "circuit." The circuit assemblies run for three days, in which the "circuit overseer" and other well-known speakers from the local area give talks from early morning to late afternoon, with a few "dramas" or skits interspersed to break up the tedium. A high point for me was being the featured piano accompanist for the Colorado Springs circuit assembly in the fall of 1982.

District conventions are usually held in larger convention halls or stadiums capable of seating from twenty to fifty thousand people, and are attended by the one hundred or more congregations that make up a "district." The district conventions run for four days and are similar to the circuit assemblies in format, with a few exceptions. Speakers at the district conventions, while drawn predominantly from the local area, often are members of the world headquarters staff in Brooklyn, New York, and sometimes even include members of the Governing Body of Jehovah's Witnesses. The high points of the district conventions for the attendees are the greatly anticipated "new releases" of Watchtower Society books, booklets, and cassette tapes. In prior years, things would often get out of hand as the many thousands of excited Witnesses swarmed the literature counters after the announcement of a new release. To alleviate this problem, new releases can no longer be purchased at the conventions, but must be purchased later at the local Kingdom Halls.

If this chronicling of Watchtower life is perhaps beginning to get a little tedious to the reader, be assured that it is often much, much more so for the Witness who is living it! In all my studying, attending meetings, preaching from door to door, conducting home "Bible" studies, filling out time reports, attending circuit assemblies and district conventions, etc., etc., I was never able to actually attain the peace of mind and the assurance of Jehovah's approval on my life that I so desperately sought. Jehovah's Witnesses have no assurance of salvation. But then, even during those very difficult years of working for "God's organization" and for my own salvation, seeds of hope and light were being sown in my heart.

4

Seeds of Truth

As mentioned earlier, during my seven-year involvement with Jehovah's Witnesses, I can't remember ever receiving a Christian witness at any of the hundreds of doors that I called on in my door-to-door work. I did, however, receive at least twelve "incidental" witnesses from Christians that I came in contact with in my everyday life.

The very first time I can remember coming in contact with evangelical (born-again) Christians was during my freshman year at Clarkson. By this time I was heavily involved with Eastern teachings, and had just been introduced to Transcendental Meditation. I saw a poster tacked up on a bulletin board on campus inviting all those interested in TM to attend an introductory meeting at Potsdam State University. My curiosity was aroused, and I attended the meeting with a friend from Clarkson.

The meeting was put on by two teachers of Transcendental Meditation. They carefully explained some of the history of TM and the "scientific" aspects of the technique, and invited all in attendance to consider paying the required sixty dollars and continuing on through the initiation ceremony. Many questions were asked, and by the end of the meeting, most of us in attendance were interested enough to take the next step.

Before the meeting concluded, two male college students who had up until this time been sitting quietly, began asking the teachers "religious" questions, such as whether TM was a religion, whether it conflicted with the teachings of Jesus, the Bible, etc. One of the students quoted the Bible, the first of the Ten Commandments: "I am the LORD your God, who brought you out of the land of Egypt, out of the house of slavery. You shall have no other gods before Me (Deut. 5:6,7)." The Christians then began asserting that Transcendental Meditation was in fact a religion, and that it was incompatible with the teachings of the Bible. Although I had by this time begun reading the Bible myself, I wrote these two Christians off as simply being too "human" to understand the more spiritual aspects of Eastern religion.

A year later, after having practiced TM for many months, I attended another, similar introductory TM meeting. Again there were several Christians present to challenge the TM instructor; one of them handed out printed sheets to each in attendance. On the sheet was a listing of seventeen TM "mantras" (a mantra is a special word repeated over and over during meditation) and the actual meaning of each of the Sanskrit words. I was startled to see my own secret mantra on the sheet, together with an English translation of the Sanskrit "puja," the hymn of worship which is recited by the TM instructor at the initiation ceremony, in which the instructor repeatedly "bows down" in worship to a host of Hindu gods and teachers, including Mahareshi's own teacher, Guru Dev.

A couple of weeks after the first introductory TM meeting, I saw another flyer posted inviting anyone interested in TM to attend an IV (InterVarsity Christian Fellowship) meeting on the Potsdam State University campus. I knew nothing about IV, but I was interested in anything having to do with with Transcendental Meditation, so I decided to attend the meeting.

When I arrived, I was surprised to find that the meeting was being held in a large lecture hall. There were perhaps two to three hundred students in attendance. An older gentleman presided over the meeting. At one point in his talk, in which he thoroughly condemned TM as being of the devil, he asked, "Will all those present who have given their lives to Jesus Christ please stand up!" All but a very few people stood up. While the speaker continued, lavishing praise upon all those who were on their feet, I sat there in my seat, terribly humiliated. Several others who were sitting eventually got up and walked out. I would have done the same, but I was just too embarrassed to get up in front of the crowd. The Christians eventually sat down and the lecture continued, though I couldn't concentrate for the rest of the meeting. I was thankful when the meeting finally ended, and I exited the hall quickly. I began practicing TM shortly thereafter.

I mentioned Don, the Christian in my dormitory hall at Clarkson, in the first chapter. In our discussions, Don had often expressed disapproval with my practicing TM, but never could seem to give me a solid reason for doing so. A year later, after I had begun studying the Bible with Jehovah's Witnesses, he again disapproved, but likewise could furnish no good reason for this. He did invite me on several occasions to his "prayer meetings," which were being held in his dorm room each week, but I declined his invitations. I would often see several students going in and out of his room with guitars on these "prayer meeting" nights, and I felt uncomfortable with this. I just wanted to learn the Scriptures! I often questioned Don about Biblical things, but it was soon apparent to me that he was not at all equipped to do battle with Jehovah's Witnesses. On the other hand, once each week, like clockwork, Marshall came right to my dorm room and studied the Scriptures with me. I studied with Marshall each week for three years, until my graduation from Clarkson in the spring of 1980.

After graduation, having moved to Colorado, I lived in a small apartment in Manitou Springs for several months. Then one day in July, a gentleman named Dwane who was in his mid-forties responded to an ad that I had placed in

the paper for a dirt bike (motorcycle). He ended up pur-
chasing the bike, and before he left he asked me, "How
much do you pay for rent here?" I answered, "$140 a
month. Why?" He said, "My permanent home is in
California. I have a house here in Manitou that my family
and I use one month each summer for vacation. We're looking for someone to stay in the house year 'round to keep an
eye on things. If you're interested, I think we could even
beat the rent that you're paying now." Of course I was
interested, and after a couple of weeks of working with
Dwane, his wife June, and their two young daughters ren-
ovating the house's downstairs apartment, I moved in. I
lived there for a little over three years.

Dwane and his family were Seventh-Day Adventists.
Each summer they would fly out to their Colorado home
and spend a full month relaxing there in the foothills of the
beautiful Rocky Mountains. One of my favorite pastimes
was dirt biking in the mountains, and Dwane (with the
motorcycle that I'd sold him) and I would often take day-
long rides together through the hundreds of miles of trails
that encircle Pikes Peak. Especially on these rides, and
sometimes at home, Dwane and I would talk about God.
The awesome scenery about us often moved us to heartfelt
expressions of thanksgiving to our Creator.

Dwane and I spent many, many hours discussing the
Sabbath, which he asserted was still binding on Christians
today. Neither of us made much headway on this topic. We
also often discussed the "last days," which Dwane seemed
to be more interested in than the average "Christian" that
I met going from door to door. However, when stumped by
a question, he would often startle me by asking his wife,
"June, what do we believe about . . . ?" How, I wondered,
could he ask someone else what *he* believed?

Dwane believed in the Trinity. Once when I asked him to
explain it, he responded, "Well, I picture the Trinity as a
committee of three Persons that always agrees on everything." I don't remember ever getting into the Scriptures
with Dwane on this topic. On another occasion, while driv-

ing down an old mountain road at night with our two dirt bikes in the back of his pickup truck, Dwane made an interesting comment. "We can be sure," he said, "that of all that God has that is of importance to us, Satan has his own counterfeit of it." I heartily agreed with him.

The overall result of our Bible discussions was summed up by Dwane one evening during the last year of my residence in Colorado: "We may not agree on a lot of things," he said, "but one thing's for sure; you've gotten our family back to the Bible."

After six months of buying, refurbishing, and selling used cars for a living, I got a production job at International Solar, a solar energy company, with the prospect of moving into a research and development position a few months down the road. There was a young fellow about my age in the production area named Ben. I eventually learned that he was a "born again" Christian, and thereafter engaged him in many theological debates. Our debates were often highly spirited, and heard by all of our fellow employees, as Ben and I worked in different departments and had to shout our arguments across the shop. I particularly enjoyed hammering Ben on the "kingdom," to which he would always respond, "The kingdom of God is not eating and drinking but righteousness, peace, and joy in the Holy Spirit" (Rom 14:17). I never did understand what he meant by this.

After working at International Solar for six months, a Witness friend, who was studying to be a stock broker, offered to sell me his mobile automotive interior repair business. I accepted his offer, and soon thereafter became the self-employed owner/operator of Colorite Interiors. I traveled in a van to most of the major car dealers in Colorado Springs (and a few in Denver) once each week and did interior repairs on their used cars. I continued operating Colorite for two years, until I sold the business in 1983.

Another Christian witness that I received at this time came from my younger brother Brad. He had become a

Christian during his freshman year at Cornell University. He came out to visit me in Colorado in January of 1981. Brad worked Colorite Interiors with me for a couple of days and we did some skiing.

Brad's and my Bible discussions at this time were disappointingly fruitless. Being a new Christian, Brad's Bible knowledge was very limited, and I, having been thoroughly trained for several years in refuting orthodox Christianity, easily shot down all of his arguments. But even so I found myself in a no-win situation. No matter how many Bible verses I fired at Brad, he still claimed that he "knew Jesus personally" and that he was "saved."

Brad, frustrated with the results of his witnessing efforts, returned home. He sent me a Christian music cassette tape and encouraged me to listen to it. I listened to part of the tape, wrote it off as "emotionalism," and didn't give it a second thought. "We're praying for you," Brad wrote to me. "Isn't that nice," I thought to myself sarcastically. "Brad and his church praying for me. What a waste of time."

Dean and I received an interesting witness one evening at a Nautilus fitness center in Colorado Springs. We had just finished our workouts, and were in the shower, preparatory to our ritual "mellowing out" in the jacuzzi. I was minding my own business, taking my shower, when the naked young man across from me turned and asked me, "Are you saved?" Dean left quickly, not wanting to get involved, but I stayed to talk with this young man, intrigued that he would ask me, a stranger, such a question. "Well," I answered him, "I'd like to think that I'm saved; I'm one of Jehovah's Witnesses." "Oh," he said. "You're not saved." That remark irked me, and we entered into a lively discussion. I don't remember what all we discussed, but I do remember that the shower stall emptied quickly, and others who came in during our discussion also left quickly. Afterwards, in the jacuzzi, I remarked to Dean how amazed I was at the boldness of this "born again" guy. And he didn't even have "the Truth!" We both agreed that we, as Jehovah's Witnesses, ought to be at least as bold as the "born agains."

Finally, I had a very interesting experience with Steve Johnson, a gentleman in his mid-thirties, who purchased a car from me. We were in my apartment writing out and signing the bill of sale, when he spotted my library of Watchtower books. "Are you a Jehovah's Witness?" he asked. I answered, "Yes." He continued, "How would you like to come up to my place some evening and have dinner with my family and me? I'd love to discuss the Bible with you." This was certainly a novel idea! "Sure," I said. "When would be a good time?" "How about this Thursday, around 5:30 or so?" "Great!" We finished the bill of sale, and Steve gave me directions to his house in Woodland Park, a short drive up Ute Pass from Manitou Springs.

Thursday evening I drove to Steve's home, tucked back in a canyon in the foothills of Pike's Peak. I met his wife and young daughter, and we had a delicious dinner. After dinner, Steve and I opened our Bibles and entered into a deep, earnest discussion of the Scriptures. At one point in our discussion, Steve asked me, "What do you see as the major theme of the Bible?" I replied, "God's kingdom." Steve's heart sank, and he said to me with glassy eyes, "Do you know what I see everywhere I turn in this book? I see Christ." I agreed with Steve that Jesus was talked about often in the Bible, but I wasn't about to succumb to his emotionalism. After three or four hours of discussion, I assured Steve that he had not budged me from my understanding of the Scriptures, but that I appreciated his inviting me over to talk with him. He was certainly an uncommon sort of "Christian!" I left his house, happy that my faith had not been shaken by him. As for Steve, I labeled him as a "goat," set in his ways, and slated for destruction at Armageddon.

In the spring of 1985 I happened to come in contact with a friend of Steve's who filled me in on some things that had transpired since our meeting in Woodland Park. Though I had completely written Steve off and hadn't given him a second thought, Steve had come to his weekly Bible study a few days following our visit, extremely disturbed. "He's so lost in that thing," he told the group, "I just couldn't reach him." So that day, Steve's Bible study group began praying for my salvation. And this they continued, earnestly, for the next four years.

5

Increasing Doubts

$\mathbf{B}$y the summer of 1982, having weathered the five years of witnessing by "born-again" Christians and having been an active part of the Foothills congregation for two and a half years, I nevertheless found myself heading downhill spiritually. Again, as in the beginning, questions were surfacing. I still believed that our Watchtower doctrine was airtight, but I found myself again having trouble with the literature.

The material in our study articles was always extremely one-sided—always presented from the rigid, unflinching Watchtower perspective. I began to wonder whether this one-sided approach to our studies offered us any means by which to evaluate the validity of any opposing viewpoints. Were we not, in fact, strictly forbidden to entertain any viewpoints that might conflict with those of the Watchtower? The Watchtower's, and therefore our own purpose in our studies, was always to simply prove ourselves right. How could we ever be fully assured of "the Truth" under these circumstances? I felt a bit off balance.

An example will illustrate the Watchtower approach to "the Truth." A couple of years following his baptism, my brother Steve, an intelligent and very studious person, began to have questions regarding the correctness of the

Watchtower's teaching on the Trinity. How did he deal with this situation? Over a period of a few months, he compiled a several-hundred-page study on the subject. This study, then, served to quell his mind on the Trinity. The study, however, was composed solely of quotations from Watchtower publications! Quotations from reputable Trinitarian scholars were only cited as they happened to be contained in the quoted Watchtower material. There was no independently researched material in his study. This was the way we were taught to think: if we had a problem or a question, we were to look to our "mother" organization for security. Only "mother" could take care of us.

Our "spiritual food" was always served predigested by the "faithful and discreet slave class." These men's interpretations of the Scriptures were always presented in the literature as irrefutable fact. This was so even though their viewpoints changed from time to time on various issues, such as on their understanding of the "superior authorities" of Romans 12, the acceptability of vaccinations, and the Witnesses' proper conduct toward those who had disassociated themselves from the Organization. We were not allowed to question the Society on these or any other points of doctrine, but were taught only to "not run ahead of God's organization." I remember a Sunday morning Watchtower study in which the Organization was likened to a ship "tacking in the wind," changing course now and then, but making steady progress toward its final destination. "The light gets brighter and brighter . . ."

Also, after these two and a half years at the Foothills congregation, I began to see that I had perhaps been wrong in staying at Foothills for so long. I didn't fit well into any of the established cliques in the congregation, and finally decided that it was time to make a move. I began attending the Mesa congregation meetings, which were held at the same Kingdom Hall, and felt somewhat more at home there. But after another six months things were still not going well. I needed a stronger change. I was growing tired of my interior repair business, and that fall I decided to move on. I sold my business to a couple of "pioneer" sisters in the Mesa congregation and moved to San Diego, California. During my two years of operating Colorite, I had developed a new method for repairing cracked dashboards, and after much prayer and an exploratory motorcycle trip to the area, I was confident that I could make a living repairing dashboards in the San Diego area.

To my dismay I found myself becoming even more miserable in San Diego. I knew no one in the area and I dearly missed my friends in Colorado. Was this where God really wanted me? Why wasn't I happy here? The dashboard business was doing fairly well, I was living in one of the most desirable cities in the country, I was one of Jehovah's Witnesses, and yet still something wasn't right!

Late one November evening, toward the end of my first month in San Diego, I took a walk along the shore of Mission Beach. It was then that I finally reached my breaking point. Alone in the dark with the sand and the seashore, I knelt on the beach and poured my heart out to my God. "Jehovah," I prayed, my heart heavy with grief, "are you really there? Why do you never answer me when I pray? Don't you know that I've given the past six years of my life to you? Don't you know the humiliation I've gone through for you, the difficulties with my parents and friends, the rebukes from the people at the doors, the man with the scissors, the late-night studies? Jehovah, don't you see these things? Don't you care about me? Don't you love me? I've worked so hard for you these past six years, and I've received not one word of encouragement from you. Have I not sought first your kingdom? Why have you given me no assurance that I'm all right with you? Jehovah, if you can, if you will, please help me!" Despairing within myself at my own lack of faith and trust in Jehovah, I threw myself upon His mercy. The next move, should there be one, was His to make.

A few days later I received a phone call from my Mom back in Hyde Park. During our conversation, she happened to mention that one of the salespeople at Taylor Manu-

facturing in Poughkeepsie was leaving the company. I
expressed interest in the vacant position, and a few days
later my Dad, vice president and sales manager of Taylor,
called me back. After talking with me for awhile, my Dad
agreed to discuss the possibility of my filling the spot with
the others at the company.

While waiting for my Dad's response, life in San Diego
was becoming unbearable. I soon packed up and moved to
Denver, and stayed there with Steve (the friend who had
sold Colorite to me) and his family for a couple of weeks.
Then came my Dad's response. A job offer! After a couple of
days of meditation and prayer, I accepted. Could this be
Jehovah's answer to my San Diego plea? I thought so. Back
in New York I would have a new job, and would be part of
the strong Hyde Park congregation. My brother Steve
would be there, too, having recently been transferred from
Brooklyn Bethel to Watchtower Farm in Wallkill, as would
be another fifteen or twenty strong "Farm brothers," most
of whom I already knew from my previous years in Hyde
Park. Things were indeed looking up! I made the move
back to New York in December of 1983, full of anticipation.

Unfortunately, though, hope for a quick spiritual renew-
al was dashed soon after my arrival in Hyde Park. The
brothers and sisters in the congregation were wonderful,
and it was good to be back together with Steve again, but
still not all was going smoothly for me. The nagging questions that I had had about the Society's indoctrination
methods were still there, and in addition, I began feeling
strangely ill at ease with some of the Society's doctrinal
stances. By this time I had read the New World
Translation from cover to cover four times, and had especially come to love the "Greek Scriptures," the New
Testament. As I continued in my daily study and Bible
reading, I began to see that the early Christians placed
more emphasis upon the person of Jesus than we did as
Jehovah's Witnesses. To make sure that this was in fact the
case, I made some comparisons and found that the ratio of
the use of Jehovah's name to the use of Jesus' name in the

Watchtower literature was ten times that of the ratio in the New Testament (I still thought the New World Translation Committee was correct in inserting the name "Jehovah" 273 times in their New Testament). At the same time I discovered that the Watchtower literature placed 27 times more emphasis on preaching than does the New Testament.

Another point bothered me. The Society had always extolled its 6% annual rate of increase as strong evidence of Jehovah's blessing on the Organization. But was this necessarily so? Now in sales, I found myself even so bold as to look at the Watchtower Society from a business standpoint. Here I saw a corporation, manufacturing its product (printed materials) with virtually free labor, and distributing it worldwide via three million zealous salespeople who worked for free! With so many active recruiters, and an income of two million dollars per week from the sale of magazines alone, was a 6% yearly increase such a strong evidence of God's blessing? This didn't seem to be a necessary conclusion.

I began to have concerns about the general selfishness of Watchtower doctrine. By this time I had read quite a number of the Society's "deeper" books, such as *Babylon the Great Has Fallen* and *The Finished Mystery,* expositions of Revelation, and *The Nations Shall Know that I Am Jehovah,* an exposition of Ezekiel. In these books in particular I found that the Watchtower interpretations of prophecy were often extremely far-fetched, always showing their fulfillments in "God's modern-day organization," Jehovah's Witnesses. My mind would often go back to a study that we had had several years earlier, in the *God's Kingdom of a Thousand Years Has Approached* book, in which Paul's vision, recorded in chapter 12 of 2 Corinthians, was discussed. According to the Society, when Paul was caught up to the third heaven, into Paradise, and heard "unutterable words, which are not lawful for a man to speak (NWT)," he was shown the "spiritual paradise," the modern-day estate of Jehovah's

Witnesses on earth! Of this he was not allowed to speak! I never could accept this ridiculous interpretation. Why couldn't the Society just let Paul have a vision from God that concerned things more wonderful than we can know right now? Why drag the Organization into it?

I began to see Watchtower selfishness also in our view of other people, especially Christian people. According to the Watchtower, of all those who heard the "good news of Jehovah's established (since 1914) kingdom" preached by Jehovah's Witnesses, not one would be saved but those who responded favorably to this teaching. How different from the first-century disciples who simply "believed on the Lord Jesus" (Acts 16:31) for salvation!

As a member of the "great crowd," I was taught that the "Christian Greek Scriptures" were not written to me; they applied directly only to the "144,000." Taking this teaching to heart made reading the "Greek Scriptures" extremely difficult. Very little applied to me directly, and I had to rely upon the Organization to sort out which Scriptures did and which did not apply to me. I was not in the "new covenant" by virtue of Christ's blood, and I knew by personal experience that I didn't have the same kind of personal relationship with Christ as did the first-century disciples. From the Society's viewpoint, I was exactly where I was supposed to be. But then, what if, God forbid, the Society was wrong? I knew I wasn't a first-century-type Christian. I hadn't been born again. I had no "heavenly hope."

In my reading of the Scriptures I began to see that the New Testament was Christ-intensive, whereas the Watchtower was Christ-passive. According to the Watchtower, Jesus, in coming to earth and dying for Adam's sin, had done his job; now it was up to us to do ours. Somehow, this "lack of Jesus" at the Kingdom Hall began to bother me more than anything else. In thinking about this one meeting night at the Hall, I opened to the index of our new songbook, *Sing Praises to Jehovah,* and discovered that only 7 of our 225 songs were about Jesus. Only 3%![84] Was something out of balance here?

I eventually began to wonder also about Watchtower chronology, particularly the teaching that Christ had returned invisibly in the year 1914. Our chronology was based on the idea that Jerusalem was taken into Babylonian captivity by Nebuchadnezzar in the year 607 B.C.E., but I had heard from my brother Steve, among others, that most scholars set the date twenty years later, at 587 B.C.E. Also, Scripture verses such as "as the lightning shines from one part of the sky to the other part of the sky, so will the coming of the Son of Man be" (Matt 24:27) and "every eye will see him" (Rev 1:7) began to trouble me.

With these questions and others growing in my mind, my "field service" was suffering. I remember approaching a house in Hyde Park with my brother Steve, and thinking to myself, "How can I teach these people that Jesus came invisibly in 1914 when I'm not absolutely sure of it myself?" James 3:1 haunted me: "Not many of you, brethren, should become teachers, for we shall incur stricter judgment."

Of course, I kept all of these questions and doubts to myself, as do all faithful Jehovah's Witnesses. I had to put up a front of "spirituality" so as not to "stumble" my brothers with these things. In addition to this was the terrible fear of disfellowshipping, the punishment for those who entertain ideas contrary to Watchtower teaching.

Finally, these inner conflicts became too much to bear. At my request, Bob and Jamie, two elders of the Hyde Park congregation, and my brother Steve, met with me in Steve's room at the Farm. After asking questions and explaining my reservations to the elders, they gave me their startling response: "We can't answer your questions. You're an intelligent individual, and quite frankly, you know the Truth as well as we do. We can't furnish you with anything that you haven't already received from the Society. We're afraid you're on your own; you're going to have to figure these things out for yourself."

Now I was in a terrible spot! I had apparently exhausted

the Society's teachings on all major points of doctrine and was still left hanging. What to do now?

A week or so later, Steve and I were in a Christian bookstore. I happened to pick up *The Companion Bible* and was leafing through it. "That's supposed to be a pretty good Bible," Steve said. "The Society quotes from it sometimes." That was all the encouragement I needed! The Bible was full of notes, and I thought that with caution, of course, these notes might help me out of my situation. I bought it, brought it home, and began reading.

Also about this time, my brother Brad had invited Jon, his pastor, to get together with me to debate the Trinity. I heartily agreed to the discussion, figuring that it would be good for Brad to see his pastor floundering in a futile attempt to defend the "Babylonish" Trinity. We got together twice, the first time with just Brad, Jon and me present, the second time with Steve joining us. For me, the meetings accomplished two unexpected things. First, I saw that for some people the Trinity doctrine is not just something that Christendom had adopted from Babylonian paganism without thought, but was indeed a doctrine that could be admirably defended from Scripture. Previous to these meetings, I was of the opinion, as are most Jehovah's Witnesses, that belief in the Trinity was just pure stupidity. After this pastor's articulate defense, however, I could no longer say that. Jon was a man, a born-again Christian man, who had *reasons* for believing in the Trinity. Second, the pastor said something in passing that somehow managed to wedge itself into my heart, never to be removed. I was explaining to the pastor how arrogant it was for a "Christian" to say that he "is saved," as though no matter what he did in his life, he would remain saved. "How much more arrogant," Jon responded, "to say that we need to add to the work of Christ, as though what He did on the cross was not sufficient for us."

Finally, with all these questions still going unanswered, and with tremendous pressure to conform to Watchtower doctrine on the one hand, and "born-again" Christians witnessing to me on the other, I finally came to the point where I had to make what was, for a Jehovah's Witness, a very radical decision. I decided to undergo a very thorough, objective, personal study of the Bible without the aid of Watchtower publications. My conviction was that if the Watchtower Society was in fact God's organization, which I still believed it was, that Jehovah God Himself would show this to me plainly through an honest, objective study of His Word.

I made my decision known to Steve, who promptly informed the Hyde Park elders. That Sunday at the Kingdom Hall, Bob, one of the elders with whom I'd met at the Farm, asked me to join him out in his car in the parking lot. In his car he questioned me as to what I was planning to do, and I freely explained it to him. He was, after all, the one who had told me that I'd have to answer my questions for myself. "I can't forbid your doing the study, Kevin," he said, "but for the sake of all of us, take care of it quickly."

So that afternoon commenced the most arduous, the most difficult period of my young life. For the next five months I searched the Scriptures four to fourteen hours a day, my eternal destiny all the while hanging in the balance.

6

The Study

Having made up my mind to do the study, I was immediately faced with a formidable problem. How does one go about doing an "objective" study of the Bible? The Watchtower method was obviously out of the question. I'd already decided not to use Watchtower literature, except as reference material, in my study. But the Watchtower's "read the paragraph, ask the question at the bottom of the page, underline the answer in the paragraph" method was the only one that I knew! What to do? I had to come up with something on my own.

As a start, I decided to read through an independent translation of the New Testament (by this point I wasn't sure whether I could trust the New World Translation) and write down all of the Scripture verses that I was having trouble with. I did this, using the New American Standard Bible, and came up with a list of two hundred verses. I then compiled these verses into fifty-eight subjects: the deity of Christ, the personality of the Holy Spirit, the great crowd, the 144,000, the year 1914, the rapture, hellfire, how to be saved, etc. Then, after reading through what I had compiled, the gravity of what I had just done hit me like a ton of bricks. I had now succeeded in destroying all of my deepest convictions concerning God, His people, the outworking of His plan of salvation, and my place in this whole affair. I was now undeniably, utterly lost!

I was still convinced, however, of three things. I knew that the Bible was God's inspired Word. I also knew that God must have people on this earth who worshiped Him in spirit and in truth (John 4:24). And I still believed that God cared for us, and that He had sent His Son Jesus here to die for us. These things were enough to convince me that God would, as Jesus had promised in John 16:13, lead even me into "all the truth."

In earnest prayer I pleaded with God. "Jehovah," I prayed, "I've torn your book apart! Please, my God, help me to put it back together again. Explain to me what You've written. I acknowledge my helplessness in this situation. Jehovah, should You see fit to lead me out of this mess, I vow that all honor and glory for this will be returned to You. Please, my God, save me from this terrible state of confusion!" And I trusted Jehovah, that He would, in His own way, in His due time, assure me of the truth that I so desperately sought.

I reread the New Testament, this time using the Revised Standard Version. I divided each of the fifty-eight topics into two sections each; one section for all the verses that I could find that seemed to support the Society's viewpoint on each subject, and the other for those that were seemingly antagonistic to it. I then read the New Testament again, this time the New International Version, and continued filling out the two sections for each subject. I repeated this a third time, using the New American Standard Bible.

As I compared the various translations of these compiled verses, checking each crucial verse with two Greek interlinears and a Greek lexicon, my confidence in the New World Translation began to wane. Time after time I discovered what appeared to be deliberate mistranslations in the text of the NWT, particularly regarding the identity of Jesus. A few examples should suffice: "they will certainly look to *the One* (Heb. Me) whom they pierced through"

(Zech 12:10); "But when he again brings his First-born into the inhabited earth, he says: 'And let all God's angels *do obeisance* (Gr. worship-see NWT, Heb 1:6 footnote) to him'" (Heb 1:6; see also Matt 2:2, 8, 11, 14:33, John 9:38); "In [the] beginning the Word was, and the Word was with God, and the Word was *a god* (Gr. God was the Word)" (John 1:1); "Jesus said to them: 'Most truly I say to you, Before Abraham came into existence, *I have been* (Gr. I am-cp. Ex 3:14, LXX)'" (John 8:58); "who, although he was existing in God's form, *gave no consideration to a seizure, namely, that he should be equal to God* (Gr. who in [the] form of God subsisting not robbery deemed [it] to be equal with God)" (Phil 2:6); "Christ, because it is in him that all the fullness of the *divine quality* (Gr. Deity or Godhead) dwells bodily" (Col 2:8-9). I found similar discrepancies in the NWT on verses which explain the Christian requirements for salvation (John 17:3, Rom 10:9-10, Heb 13:15), the Christian's personal relationship with Christ (1 Cor 1:9, 2 Cor 11:3, 2 Cor 13:5, 1 John 1:3) and many other verses on other important topics (Matt 5:18, Matt 27:52-53, Acts 5:3, 2 Cor 11:8, Eph 4:24, Col 3:10, Heb 12:23, etc.). Regarding the insertion by the New World Translation committee of the name "Jehovah" into the text of the New Testament, the Watchtower's own statement should suffice: "Why, then, do all extant copies of the 'New Testament' lack the Tetragrammaton?" (WT 5/1/78, p. 10). All things considered, I found the New World Translation to be sorely mistranslated in accordance with the preconceived theology of its biased and unscrupulous translators.

Although I knew virtually nothing of the science of Biblical hermeneutics at the time, I soon realized something that revolutionized my understanding of the Scriptures. I began to see, much to my amazement, that the great majority of Bible passages made perfect sense if I simply took them literally, provided there were no indications within the texts themselves that I should do otherwise. Suddenly passages involving the still unfulfilled prophecies given to the nation Israel in the Old Testament

(Gen 13:14, 15, Is 2:1-4, 11:9,11-12, 66:20, 22, Jer 33:14-16, Amos 9:14, 15, Zech 14:3, 4, 16, 17, etc.), the "rapture" verses (1 Thess 4:15-17), and verses describing the second coming of Christ ("every eye will see him," Rev 1:7) began to take on wonderful new meaning. I was learning the beauty of the "grammatico-historical method" of Bible interpretation: If the plain sense of Scripture makes good sense, seek no other sense! What's more, discarding the Watchtower's often fanciful "spiritualized" interpretations in favor of taking the Bible at face value began to make the help of the Watchtower's "faithful and discreet slave" superfluous. If I could read the Bible, take it literally, and understand it, what need was there for the "faithful slave class"?

Here are the conclusions that I came to after five months of intensive study:[85]

God

Jehovah is the only true God (undisputed).

Jesus is the creator (Gen 1:26-27, Is 44:24, John 1:3, Rom 11:36, John 1:10, Eph 3:9, Col 1:15-16 [cp. Ps 89:27, Gen 41:51-52, Jer 31:9], Heb 1:8,10, 3:3-4) and sustainer (Col 1:17, Heb 1:3) of all things. He is the Savior (Is 43:11, Is 45:21, Hos 13:4, Titus 1:3-4, 2:13, 3:4, Titus 3:6, 2 Pet 1:1). He gives things that only God can give (John 1:12-13, Rev 2:23). He is the judge of all (John 5:22-23, 2 Cor 5:10) and has authority to forgive sins (Mark 2:5-7,10, Luke 5:21, 5:24, 1 Cor 8:12, Eph 4:32). He is all-seeing (1 Ki 8:39, Rev 2:23), omniscient (1 Ki 8:39, Matt 9:4, 12:25, Mark 2:8, Luke 6:8, 9:47, John 11:1, Col 2:2-3, Rev 2:23 [cp. 1 Ki 8:39]), and omnipresent (Matt 18:20, 28:20). Jesus was eternally preexistent (Micah 5:2, John 1:1, Col 1:17, Heb 7:3) and He never changes (Heb 1:8,10, 13:8). It is proper to serve Him (John 12:26, Rom 1:1, 1 Cor 4:1, 2 Cor 5:15, Gal 1:10, Phil 1:1, Col 3:24, 4:12, Jas 1:1, Jude 1), to pray to Him (John 14:14 [Kingdom Interlinear], Acts 7:59-60, 9:14, 9:20-21, 22:16, 22:17-19, Rom 10:9, 11-13, 1 Cor 1:2, 2 Cor 12:8-9, 1 Ti 1:12, Rev 22:20), to give Him glory (Is 42:8,

48:11, Dan 7:13-14, John 1:14, 5:22-23, 11:4, 13:31-32, 16:13-15, 17:5, Acts 3:13, Phil 2:9, Col 1:16, 2 Thess 1:12, 2 Pet 3:18, Rev 1:5-6, 5:11-14), and to worship Him (Matt 2:2,8,11, 4:10, 14:33, 28:9,16-17, John 9:38, Heb 1:6, Rev 5:8, 14:7 [cp. Acts 10:25, Rev 19:10, 22:8-9]). Jesus is Lord (Deut 10:17, Matt 12:8, John 20:27-28, Rom 10:9,11-13, Eph 4:4-5, James 2:1, Rev 17:14, 19:16) and is sovereign with His Father (Matt 25:31, 28:18, John 3:31,35, 13:3, 16:15, 17:10, Phil 2:9-11, Heb 1:2, 2:8, Rev 22:3). Being the Son of God (John 5:18, 10:28-33,36), He is also truly God (Deut 32:36,39, Is 9:6, 10:21, 43:10, 44:6 [cp. Is 48:12, Rev 1:17-18, 2:8, 21:6-7, 22:12-16,20], Matt 1:23, 13:41, John 1:1, 2:19,21 [cp. Acts 2:24], 5:18, 8:19,28,58-59 [cp. Ex 3:14; LXX], 10:28-33, 12:44, 13:19, 14:7-9, 15:13, 18:4-6, 20:28-29, Acts 20:28, Eph 3:19, Phil 2:6, Col 2:9, 1 Ti 3:15-16, Titus 2:13, Heb 1:3-4,8 [cp. Ps 45:6], 3:1-4, 2 Pet 1:1, 1 John 5:20, Rev 22:1-4) and Jehovah (Zech 2:8-11, 11:12-13 [cp. Matt 26:14-15], 12:1,10 [cp. Rev 1:7], 14:3-5 [cp. Matt 25:31, Acts 1:11-12], 14:5 [cp. 1 Thess 3:13], Matt 3:3, Mark 1:2-3, Luke 3:4, John 1:23, Luke 1:76 [cp. Is 40:3], Matt 21:15-16 [cp. Ps. 2:6], John 17:11-12, Rom 10:9,11-13 [cp. Joel 2:32], Phil 2:9, 1:4, 1:8,10 [cp. Ps 102:22-25]), together with His Father.

The Holy Spirit is a Person (Matt 3:16, 10:20, Mark 1:10, Luke 12:12, John 1:32, 14:16-17,26, 15:26, 16:7-8,13-15, Acts 1:16, 5:3,9, 10:19-20, 15:28, 20:23, Rom 8:16, 1 Cor 12:11, Eph 4:30, Heb 3:7, Heb 10:15, Rev 22:17), and is God (Gen 1:2 [cp. vs. 1], Matt 12:32, Luke 12:10, John 14:26, Acts 1:16 [cp. Heb 1:1], Acts 5:3-4, 28:25 [cp. Heb 1:1], 2 Cor 13:14, Heb 10:15-17) together with the Father and with the Son.

The Old Testament in several places indicates plurality in the Godhead (Gen 1:1-3, 1:26, 3:22, 11:7,9, Gen 18, 19:24, Ex 23:20-23 [cp. 1 Cor 10:4], Is 48:12,16, 63:7-14, Zech 2:8-11, 3:2]). As mentioned above, the Bible indicates both the deity of Christ and the personality and deity of the Holy Spirit. These factors, together with the deity of the Father (undisputed), produce a description of the Godhead in trinity. Especially in the New Testament, these three Persons are repeatedly spoken of as cooperating collectively (Matt 3:16-17, Mark 1:9-11, Luke 3:21-22, Matt 28:19, Luke 1:35, John 3:34-35, John 14:26, 16:13-15, Acts 2:32-33, 38-39, Rom 15:16,30, 1 Cor 12:4-6, 2 Cor 3:4-6, 13:14 [cp. 1 John 1:3], Gal 4:4-6, Eph 4:4-6, Heb 10:12,15, 1 Pet 1:2).

Man

Man is composed of the spirit, the soul, and the body (1 Thess 5:23).

The term "sleep" is never applied to either the spirit or the soul in the Bible, but only to the body (Ps 146:3-4, Matt 9:24, John 11:11, Acts 7:59-60, 13:36, 1 Thess 4:14).

The spirit of man is a distinct entity, and normally dwells in the body (Zech 12:1, Matt 26:41, Mark 2:8, 8:12, Luke 1:46-47, Rom 1:9, 8:16, 1 Cor 2:11, 5:5, 6:20, 14:2,14, 2 Cor 7:1, 2 Ti 4:22). At death the spirit departs from the body (Eccl 12:7, Is 26:19, Luke 8:52,55, 23:46, Acts 7:59-60, Heb 12:22-24). In this state the individual awaits resurrection of the body (Deut 18:10-11, 1 Sam 28:11-15, Eccl 12:7, Is 14:9-10, Matt 10:28, 17:3, Mark 9:4 [cp. Matt 17:9; "vision": Gr. orama—that which is seen; a spectacle-cp. Luke 24:23], Matt 27:49-50, Mark 15:36, Luke 12:5, 16:22,25,30, 23:43,46, John 2:19, 8:51, 11:25-26, 19:30, Acts 7:59, 20:10, Rom 8:38-39, 2 Cor 5:8, Phil 1:23-24, 2:10, 2 Ti 4:6, Heb 12:22-23, 2 Pet 1:13-15, Rev 6:9-11, 20:4; see also the verses cited below in reference to resurrection).

Although man in totality is often referred to in the Bible as a soul (e.g. Gen 2:7), many passages speak of the soul of man living on after the death of the body (Gen 35:18, 1 Ki 17:21-22, Matt 10:28, Acts 20:9-10, Rev 6:9-11, 20:4).

Jesus' body was resurrected (Matt 12:40, Mark 16:6, Luke 24:3,39, John 2:19,21, 20:27, Acts 2:27 [cp. Ps. 16:10], 13:34-37, Col 2:9, 1 Ti 2:5).

The bodies of Christians with the "heavenly hope" will be resurrected (Rom 8:11,23, Phil 3:20-21). Their bodies will be *changed* at their resurrection (John 20:26, 1 Cor 15:44,52-53).

At the resurrection, men will be judged by the deeds which they have performed in their bodies during their previous lives on earth; not by future deeds which they will perform during the millennium (Matt 16:27, Luke 11:31-32, John 5:28,29, Acts 17:31, 2 Cor 5:10, Heb 9:27, Rev 20:12-13).

The "second resurrection" occurs after the millennial reign of Christ has been completed (Rev 20:5 [cp. vs. 4]).

It is possible for one to experience torment in Hades (Luke 16:23-24).

Eternal, conscious torment is the eventuality of those who are cast into "gehenna," the lake of fire (Is 66:24, Dan 12:2, Matt 3:12, 8:11-12, 29, 13:42,49-50, 18:8, 22:13, 25:46, Mark 5:7, 9:43, Luke 3:17, 10:12, 12:5, Heb 10:27-29, Rev 14:9-11, 19:20, 20:10, 22:14-15).

God's People

Unfulfilled prophecy given to the nation Israel will have fulfillment in the nation Israel (Gen 3:15 [cp. 37:9,10, Rev 12:1,5], 13:14-15, 17:7-8, 2 Sam 7:16, Ps 2:6, Is 2:1-4, 11:9,11-12 [cp. Matt 24:31, Rev 7:1-8], 25:6-10, 27:6, 33:20,24, 35:5-10, 45:17, 52:1, 65:17-21,24, 66:20,22, Jer 3:17-18, 23:3-8, 33:14-16, Ez 16:60, 21:25-27, 37:25, Hos 3:5, Joel 2:32, 3:20, Amos 9:14-15, Ob 15,17, Mic 4:1-4,7, Zeph 3:8,9,14-17, Hag 2:6-7,9, Zech 2:10-12, 8:20-23, 12:9-10, 14:3-4,16-17, 14:4 [cp. Acts 1:9,11-12], Matt 5:35, 10:23, 19:28, 23:37-39, Luke 1:32-33, 13:34-35, 21:24, Acts 1:6-7, 3:19-21, Rom 11:25-29, Rev 7:4, 12:1,5 [cp. Gen 37:9-10], Rev 14:1, 20:9 [cp. Is 52:1]). The restoration and blessing of Israel is a critical element in the outworking of Jehovah's kingdom program.

Jesus, when speaking to His disciples, referred to them as a "little flock," which they were at the time (Luke 12:32). There is no basis for equating the "little flock" of Luke 12:32 with the 144,000 of Revelation chapters 7 and 14.

The 144,000 are sealed from among the nation Israel (Rev 7:3,4,9, 14:1,6) to become "bondservants of our God," in contrast with earth's millennial kings who are purchased from "every tribe and tongue and people and nation" (Rev 5:9-10). The 144,000 are sealed just prior to or during the Tribulation (Rev 7:1,3).

The Bible nowhere states that the 144,000 are sealed to be kings, priests, or the bride of Christ (Rev 7:3-8, 14:1-5).

In our day, as in the first century, God is dealing primarily with the church of Jesus Christ (Acts 20:28, 1 Cor 12:12, 2 Cor 11:2, Eph 2:21-22, 4:4, 5:29-32, 1 Ti 3:15, Heb 12:22-23).

There is no good reason for equating the "other sheep" of John 10:16 with the "great crowd" of Revelation 7:9. By all indications the "other sheep" of John 19:16 are gentile Christians (John 10:16, 11:51-52, Eph 2:13-14,16).

Members of the great crowd may or may not pass through the great tribulation and enter directly into everlasting life on earth. There are indications that they will spend some time in heaven (Rev 7:9,15,11, 14:1,3; 7:9,15, 3:12, 11:19, 15:5-6,8, 16:1, 11:1-2; 7:9,15, 13:6, 15:5-6, Heb 8:1-2, 9:11,24; Rev 7:9,14, 22:14 [cp. 21:2]).

The rapture is the only valid hope (other than dying in Christ and being resurrected) for all true Christians alive on earth today (see the verses cited below in reference to the rapture).

There is more than one faithful slave mentioned in Jesus' parables (Matt 25:20-23).

The "faithful and sensible slave" will be identified and rewarded when Christ returns (Matt 24:44-47). Christ has not yet returned (see the verses cited below in reference to the return of Christ).

The "faithful and discreet slave class" of Jehovah's Witnesses has proven to be neither faithful nor discreet in their interpretation of Bible prophecy. (The following are some of the predictions made by the "faithful and discreet slave class" of Jehovah's Witnesses over the years: The year 1799 definitely marks the beginning of the time of the end [Creation, pp. 294,298]. The 1000 years of Christ's reign began in 1873 [The Time Is at Hand, foreword p. 2]; the Scriptural proof is that the second presence of the Lord Jesus Christ began in 1874 A.D. [Prophecy, p. 65]. The second coming of the Lord began in 1874 [Creation, pp. 289,298, Prophecy, p. 76]. The beginning of the battle of the great day is dated from October 1874 [WT 1/15/1892, p. 1355]. The Kingdom of God will begin its exercise of power in 1878 [The Time Is at Hand p. 101]. The formal inauguration of Christ's kingly office dates from April 1878 [The Day of Vengeance, p. 621]. Christ has been invisibly present since October 1884 [The Day of Vengeance, p. 621]. The battle of the great day of God the Almighty had begun by 1886 [WT 1/1886, vol. VII, pp. 816,817]. The battle of the great day of God Almighty is already commenced [The Time Is at Hand (1908), p. 101]. The stress of the great time of trouble will be on us somewhere between 1910 and 1912 [The New Creation, p. 579]. World War I is leading into the Battle of Armageddon [WT 4/1/15, p. 102]. By the end of 1914 the blindness of natural Israel will begin to be turned away [The Time Is at Hand, p. 77]. The last member of the church will be glorified sometime before the end of 1914 [The Time Is at Hand, p. 77]. Christendom will be completely destroyed by October 1914 [WT 1/15/1892, p. 1355]. The year 1914 will be the farthest limit of the rule of imperfect men [The Time Is at Hand, pp. 76,77]. The date for the close of the battle of the great day is definitely marked in Scripture as October 1914 [WT 1/15/1892, p. 1355]. Armageddon is likely to begin in the spring of 1915 [WT 9/1/14]. The battle of the great day of God Almighty had begun by 1916 [WT 9/1/16, pp. 265,266]. In the year 1918 God will destroy the churches wholesale and the church members by the millions; any that escape shall come to the works of Pastor Russell to learn the meaning of the downfall of "Christianity" [The Finished Mystery, p. 485]. The date 1925 is even more distinctly indicated by the Scriptures than is 1914, and before 1925 the great crisis will be reached and probably passed [WT 9/1/22]. In

1925 the earthly phase of the Kingdom will be recognized [Millions Now Living Will Never Die, p. 89]. Abraham, Isaac, Jacob and the faithful prophets of old will be resurrected and fully restored to perfect humanity in the fall of 1925 [Millions Now Living Will Never Die, pp. 88-90]. We should, therefore, expect shortly after 1925 to see the awakening of Abel, Enoch, Noah, Abraham, Isaac, Jacob, Melchisedec, Job, Moses, Samuel, David, Isaiah, Jeremiah, Ezekiel, Daniel, John the Baptist, and others mentioned in the eleventh chapter of Hebrews [The Way to Paradise, p. 224], the remaining months before Armageddon [WT 9/15/41, p. 288]. Those faithful men of old may be expected back from the dead any day now [The New World (1942), p. 104]. Six thousand years from man's creation will end in 1975. It may be the purpose of God for Christ's reign to run parallel with the 7th millennium of man's existence [Life Everlasting in the Freedom of the Sons of God, pp. 29-30, WT 8/15/68, pp. 497-501].)

Christians are taught primarily by God's Word, the Bible, and by the Holy Spirit (Matt 16:16-17, Matt 18:20, John 14:26, 15:26, 16:13, Gal 1:15-18, 1 John 2:26-27, 1 John 5:20). Human agencies may also be employed (Acts 8:30-31).

Christians are persecuted for bearing the name of Jesus Christ (Matt 5:11, 10:22, 24:9, Mark 13:13, Luke 21:12,17, John 15:21, Acts 9:16, Gal 6:12, Phil 1:29, 2 Ti 3:12, 1 Pet 4:14,16, Rev 2:3, 16:6, 20:4).

Salvation

The true gospel is primarily the good news of our redemption by the blood of Jesus Christ, which redemption is to be appropriated by faith (1 Cor 1:17-18,23-24, 15:1-4, Col 1:19-23). The gospel preached by the apostle Paul was primarily "Christ crucified" (1 Cor 1:22-24).

The "gospel" preached by Jehovah's Witnesses is very different from that which was preached by the apostle Paul and by Christians throughout the centuries ("Let the honest-hearted person compare the kind of preaching of the gospel done by the religious systems of Christendom during all the centuries with that done by Jehovah's Witnesses since the end of World War I in 1918. They are not one and the same kind. That of Jehovah's Witnesses is really "gospel" or "good news," as of God's heavenly kingdom that was established by the enthronement of his Son Jesus Christ at the end of the Gentile Times in 1914." [Watchtower, May 1, 1981, p. 17]).

According to the Scriptures, the messengers of the gospel preached by Jehovah's Witnesses are to be accursed (Gal 1:8-9).

To be born again means to be born spiritually by a supernatural act of God (Jer 31:33-34, Ez. 36:25-27, Tit 3:5, 1 Pet 1:23).

One must be born again to be saved (John 1:12-13, Acts 2:38-39, Rom 8:8-9 [cp. vs. 15], 1 John 5,12).

One cannot see God's kingdom or enter into it without having been born again (John 3:3,5,7).

The "new man" is created in a Christian when he is born again (2 Cor 5:17, Eph 4:24-25, Col 3:9-11).

To be saved one must believe on the Lord Jesus Christ (John 3:14-16,36, 6:47, Acts 13:38-39,48, 16:29-31, Rom 10:9-10,13, Rev 3:20).

One can test himself to see whether or not he is "in the faith" (2 Cor 13:5). The indwelling Holy Spirit bears witness to a Christian that he has been saved (Rom 8:16, Eph 1:13-14). The Christian has assurance of salvation (John 5:24, 10:28, Rom 8:1-2,11, Eph 1:13-14, 4:30, Phil 4:3, Col 3:3-4, Heb 10:35, 1 John 5:13). It is proper for a Christian to say that he has been saved (John 3:36, 5:24, 6:47, Rom 5:11, 8:1-2, Eph 2:5, 4:32, Phil 4:3, 2 Ti 1:8-9, Heb 10:19, 1 Pet 1:23, 1 John 3:14, 5:11,13).

The Christian's *bodily* salvation is yet future (Rom 5:9-10, 8:11, Eph 4:30, 1 Pet 1:4-5).

The finished redemptive work of Christ is fully sufficient for the justification of a believer (Acts 13:39, Rom 8:1-2, Col 1:21-22, 2:13-14,20-23, Heb 9:12, 10:10, 1 Pet 2:24). A

Christian is justified by faith in Christ alone (John 3:16-18,36, 5:24, 6:28-29,40,47, 20:31, Acts 10:43, 13:39, 26:15,18, Rom 3:21-28, 5:1, 6:23, 7:6, 8:1-2, Gal 2:16, 5:1, Eph 2:8-9, Phil 3:9, Col 2:13-14,20-23, Titus 3:5-7, Heb 4:10, 1 John 1:7, 3:22-23, Rev 5:9, 7:14). Good works, however, naturally follow true faith (Matt 7:21-23, Eph 2:8-9, Phil 2:12-13, Titus 3:5-8, Jas 2:17,20,24,26).

One must come to Jesus for salvation (Matt 11:28-30, John 5:39-40, 6:35,37,44,45, 7:37-38, 12:32, 14:6, Heb 13:13, 1 Pet 2:25).

One can know Jesus personally (John 14:21, 17:3, Phil 3:10). One who has no relationship with Christ has no relationship with God (Gal 3:26, 1 John 5:12).

A Christian has an intimate personal relationship with Jesus (John 14:23, 15:4-5, 17:23, Rom 13:14, 1 Cor 1:9, 6:16-17, 2 Cor 12:9, 13:5, Gal 2:20, 3:27, 4:6,19, Eph 3:16-17, 4:15, Phil 4:7, Col 2:6,10, 3:11, 1 Pet 3:15, 1 John 1:3, Rev 3:20).

A Christian should love Jesus more than he loves his own life (Matt 16:25, 20:37, Eph 6:24, Phil 1:21, 3:8).

All true Christians alive today have been born again, are under the new covenant by virtue of Christ's blood, and rightly partake of the emblematic bread and wine (John 6:33,51,53, Rev 7:9,14).

Christian life, empowered by the Holy Spirit, is fundamentally free and simple (Matt 11:28-30, Acts 13:39, Rom 7:6, 14:14,17, 1 Cor 2:2, 10:23, 2 Cor 11:3, Gal 3:2-3, Heb 4:10, Titus 1:15, 1 Pet 2:16, 1 John 5:3-5). A Christian is not subject to the bondage of men who would enslave him (1 Cor 7:23, Gal 2:4-5, 5:1,13).

Although Christians are encouraged to witness to their fellow men (Matt 28:19-20, Acts 5:42, 1 Cor 9:16, 11:1, Eph 6:15, Phil 1:14, Rev 22:17), house-to-house preaching is not a prerequisite for salvation.

Christians have differing roles in the ministry; not all Christians are preachers (1 Cor 12:28-29, Eph 4:11).

The message to be preached by Christians today is "Christ crucified" (Luke 24:46-47, 1 Cor 1:23).

The Last Days

The invisible return of Christ in the year 1914 is a foundational doctrine of Watchtower theology (cp. the Watchtower's interpretations of Matt 24:45-47, 25:31-32, etc.).

The return of Christ did not occur invisibly in the fall of 1914 C.E. (Matt 24:42,44, Acts 1:6-7). This visible event is still future (Matt 24:26-27,30, Mark 13:26, Luke 17:24, 21:27, Acts 1:9,11-12 [cp. Zech 14:4], 3:21, Phil 3:20, 1 Thess 4:16, 2 Thess 1:7, 1 Ti 6:14, 2 Ti 4:8, Titus 2:13, Heb 9:28, 1 John 2:28, 3:2, Rev 1:7 [cp. Zech 12:10]).

The duration of the "times of the gentiles" cannot be ascertained by a study of Daniel chapter 4 (this prophecy was fulfilled by Nebuchadnezzar in Daniel 4:24-37).

The kingdom is restored to the nation Israel at the end of the "times of the gentiles" (see the verses cited above in reference to the future restoration of the nation Israel).

The signs of Christ's return are to occur before His return and are to give evidence that He is shortly to appear (Matt 24:7-8,33, Mark 13:29, 13:8).

We should expect to find persons in these last days prematurely announcing Christ's return (Luke 21:8-9).

The rapture has not yet occurred. At the rapture, Christians will be taken up bodily to meet the Lord (John 14:3,18, Phil 3:20-21, 1 Thess 1:10, 4:15-18, 1 John 3:2, Rev 3:10). Expectation of the rapture has a purifying affect on those who have this hope (Phil 1:6,10, 1 John 2:28, 3:2-3).

Christ will be physically present on earth during the millennium (see the verses cited above in reference to the return of Christ and the future restoration of the nation Israel). The bride of Christ will rule with Him then.

There will be those who will live through the great tribulation and enter directly into the cleansed earth (see Israel, above). Humans will inhabit the earth during the millennium. However, the rapture is the only Biblical hope for Christians alive now.

The present heaven and the present earth will be destroyed by fire at the end of the 1000-year reign of Christ (Ps 102:25-26, Is 51:6, Matt 5:18, 24:35, Mark 13:31, Luke 21:33, Heb 1:10-12, 2 Pet 3:7,10-12, Rev 20:11). A new heaven and a new earth will be created (Is 65:17, 2 Pet 3:13, Rev 21:1).

Summary

To sum up the findings of my study, historic evangelical Christianity, not Jehovah's Witnesses, is indeed the one "true religion." The Watchtower Society is, far from being "God's clean organization," one of the "false prophets" that Jesus warned us of in Matthew chapter 24. Jehovah's Witnesses are, far from being the "only true Christians," yet another entry in the age-long list of man-made rebellions against the true church of God, the "pillar and support of the truth" (1 Ti 3:15).

7

Born Again!

It was now early October of 1984. I was on a jet, on my way to Los Angeles for a business trip. I was past the midway point in my study, and the new things that my Watchtower-encrusted mind was learning from the Bible were beginning to trickle down into my heart.

We were soaring over Ohio at 35,000 feet. As I looked out the window, a city far below caught my eye, and something welled up inside me. "Jesus died for all those people down there," I thought to myself, "not just Jehovah's Witnesses." I thought of my own arrogance as I had gone from door to door preaching that no one could be saved who had rejected the Watchtower, God's organization. But now things were looking very different. It really wasn't *we* who were important, not the Watchtower, not any man, but *Christ.* It was *Jesus* who had died. It was *Jesus* who calls His sheep by name (John 10:3). And there were people down there, humble, simple people, whom Jesus dearly loved, that I had cast off as "goats," not fit to be God's people. Yes, things were beginning to look very different! Jesus and His work were taking on wonderful new meaning.

It was on this trip to Los Angeles that I first thought that I might eventually become a born-again Christian. I had amassed hundreds of Scripture verses, most of which contradicted the teachings of Jehovah's Witnesses, and I was quickly approaching the point where I'd have to begin drawing conclusions. Also, I had begun having various "coincidences" occur in my daily life that made me wonder whether the Father was somehow taking a special interest in drawing me to Jesus (John 6:44).

I stayed at a hotel in Santa Monica, and spent Saturday at the beach, studying as usual. On my walk back to the hotel, I was about to pass by an old man on a street corner, when he called to me. "Hey! Is that a Bible you've got there?" I stopped in my tracks. "Yes, it is," I said. He came over to me. "Praise the Lord, brother!" I showed him my Companion Bible. "Have you ever read Scofield?" he asked. I answered, "No." I'd never heard of Scofield. "You have to read Scofield!" he said. "Scofield's the best!" I had no idea what he was talking about. As I turned to leave, he handed me a tract, saying again, "Read Scofield!" "Okay," I said, and walked back to the hotel. "What a crazy old man," I thought to myself. Back in my room, I pulled out the tract that he had given me and looked it over. It had color comic book pictures of people burning in hell, etc. I'd been given many of these by Christians over the years. As usual, I deposited it in the trash.

A couple of weeks later, my brother Brad and I were in a Christian bookstore in Fishkill, New York. As I was looking over the Bibles, one of them caught my eye. *Scofield?* Hmm. I suddenly remembered the old man on the street corner. I picked up the *Oxford NIV Scofield Study Bible.* I was amused, as I had forgotten all about the old man. The Bible looked interesting; it was full of references and study notes. I purchased it and brought it home. I added "Scofield" to my library of reference books, and referred to him often throughout the remainder of my study.

My return flight from California was a milestone in my pilgrimage. I had finished my work in Los Angeles, and had spent the last few days of my trip in the San Francisco Bay area. I boarded a plane at the San Francisco airport and was soon heading back to New York.

I introduced myself to the woman sitting next to me on the plane. "My name's Ginny," she said. My daughter was going to be flying with me today, but she had to cancel out at the last minute, so it looks like you got her seat." We exchanged some small talk, and I found myself enjoying her company.

A half hour or so into the five-hour flight, after dozing just a bit to relax, I opened my eyes, getting ready to continue work on my study. I looked over at Ginny. She had her tray table open, and was writing in a workbook of some kind. Then I looked and saw, also open on her tray table, a *Bible!* From time to time she would look up a Scripture verse or two in her Bible, then continue writing in her workbook.

My heart began pounding. "Jehovah, what's going on here?" I prayed silently. I wanted so badly to continue in my study; I was about ready to begin drawing conclusions, and I couldn't afford to waste precious time. But I couldn't study now; Ginny would surely notice what I was doing and ask me about it. But I couldn't tell her! What if it turned out that Jehovah's Witnesses were right after all? What kind of witness would I be giving Ginny if I were to let her know anything about the terrible battle that I was going through? One of Jehovah's Witnesses with *doubts?* No, I couldn't risk it.

Oh, but I wanted to talk to her! I had kept my study secret for over four months now, and it was tearing me apart inside. I had no one on earth that I could talk about it with. Talking with any other Jehovah's Witness was out, since even my closest friends would be required to turn me in to the elders if they heard any "apostate" ideas from me. I would then be quickly disfellowshipped, cut off forever from my friends and from my brother Steve. Talking with Christians was out, because for them to hear of a Jehovah's Witness with doubts would be a horrible reproach upon Jehovah's name if it was to turn out that Jehovah's Witnesses did have the truth after all.

After three hours of this torture, Ginny and I were again

exchanging small talk. "Where are you headed once you get to New York?" I asked her. "Peekskill," she said. "Hey, what a coincidence!" I said. "I'm going to Hyde Park." Hyde Park is about thirty miles north of Peekskill, which in turn is fifty miles north of New York City. "How are you getting up there?" I asked. "I'm taking the Hudson Valley Transporter," she answered. "Wow! Me too!" We both marveled that the two of us, sitting next to each other on the plane from San Francisco, would be taking the same shuttle service to our respective upstate towns.

Ginny put away her books, and for the last hour of the flight the two of us sat in silent contemplation. My heart was aching now. Oh, how I wanted to talk to her! But no, I couldn't! There was just no way. The stakes were too high. But then I had an idea.

"Jehovah," I prayed silently, my heart thumping all the more, "I would so much like to talk with Ginny about you and about the Bible. You know all things, my God. You know that I love you, that I'd never do anything to bring your great and holy Name into reproach. Therefore I've resolved in my heart not to say a word to her about you or about my study. But, Jehovah, if by some chance she has something to share with me, then let her say something first. This situation is in your hands, Jehovah. If she says nothing, then I'll say nothing. But if she initiates a conversation about you, I'll understand that you have, in the light of this prayer, allowed her to do it, and that it is okay for me to talk to her." I felt safe with this prayer. Since I had said nothing about and had shown no interest in her Bible study, there was no reason in the world why she should start talking to me about God, except by His prompting. The situation was safely in God's hands.

We deplaned in New York and made our way to the baggage claim area. Standing together waiting for our bags to appear on the carousel, I again commented to Ginny what a coincidence it was that the two of us would be traveling upstate on the same shuttle. Then she hit me with a bombshell. "I don't think it's a coincidence," she said. My heart began pounding again. "What do you mean?" I asked, bracing myself for her answer. "Since I've come to know the Lord," she said, "I've come to understand that nothing happens by coincidence. There's a reason why my daughter canceled out at the last minute. There's a reason why we sat together on the plane, and there's a reason why we'll be traveling together on the shuttle. I think the Lord wants me to talk to you."

Well, that was it. God had opened the door, and I don't think anyone or anything in heaven or on earth could have shut it. "I'm one of Jehovah's Witnesses," I heard myself telling Ginny, "and I've been having some questions . . ." We sat on a bench in the baggage claim area, still waiting for our luggage. I pulled out my loose-leaf notebook, now almost two inches thick with study notes, and showed it to Ginny. "Now I know the Lord wants me to talk to you," she said as she dug into her carry-on bag and pulled out her Bible. Opening to Genesis 1:1, she began, "'In the beginning *God* created the heavens and the earth. . . . The *Spirit* of God was moving over the surface of the waters. Then God *said* . . .'" And there on that bench and for the next three hours during our trip on the shuttle, she spoke to me and reasoned with me from the Word of God. As it turned out, Ginny was a Bible teacher from a small town east of San Francisco. We spoke freely during our bus trip, almost oblivious to the world around us. Looking back, the other people on the bus must have gotten a real earful!

Finally it was time for Ginny to exit the bus, and we said goodbye. Before stepping off, though, Ginny turned back and gave me a final admonition. "All I ask is that you give Jesus a chance in your life," she said. "I will," I called back. "I promise you that!"

After the trip, meetings at the Kingdom Hall were never the same. The first Sunday public talk was entitled, "Is God a Trinity?" After the talk and Watchtower study, one of the "Farm brothers" asked me, "Well, what did you think of the public talk?" "Typical," was my reply. I so badly wanted to tell this brother how poor the elder's talk really was, but "typical" was as strong as I dared be. If I was to be leaving Jehovah's Witnesses, I was going to leave of my own volition. Disfellowshipping for what they considered to be "apostasy" was not on my agenda. So I continued to keep my doubts to myself. And although I was still attending all of the required meetings, I found myself able to say "amen" to very few of the prayers offered by the brothers.

By mid-November of 1984, my study had reached its final size of 218 pages, covering 82 topics and citing over 800 Scripture verses. I was beginning to draw conclusions. One topic at a time, I read, reread, and reread again all the verses pertaining to the topic, eventually holding them all in my mind at once; finally arriving at the essence of what the Scriptures taught on the subject; and writing the conclusion that I had come to at the end of the topic. I began with the simpler topics, and progressed on through the more difficult ones, leaving the three most difficult ones (for a Jehovah's Witness)—the deity of Christ, the personality of the Holy Spirit, and the Trinity—for last. Since these three doctrines were so vitally connected, I thought it best to arrive at conclusions for them simultaneously. And the day finally did arrive for a decision on these also. First was the deity of Christ. After many days of painstaking reading, sorting, meditating, and re-sorting of over two hundred fifty verses pertaining to the deity of Christ alone, holding the essence of all these verses in mind at once, I finally was able to conclude without reservation that the Bible does in fact teach that Jesus Christ is God. Conclusions on the personality of the Holy Spirit and the Trinity soon followed, and then, quite unexpectedly, there was peace. The study was finished! But I still had yet to come to Jesus personally for salvation (John 5:39-40).

The last meeting that I attended at the Kingdom Hall was the Theocratic Ministry School and Service Meeting on Friday, November 16, 1984. Before the meeting began, I approached Bob, an elder with whom I had met at the Farm and who had called me out to talk with him in his car, and requested a meeting with him and the other elders. He declined, saying that all the elders would be at the Kingdom Ministry School that weekend. He suggested that they might be able to meet with me the following weekend. "No," I said, "that will probably be too late. I'm considering disassociating myself from the Organization." Even then, Bob maintained that the weekend's plans were set and that I would have to wait. The meeting began.

My heart was on fire. The talk presented from the platform was pure blasphemy, and I had to strongly restrain myself from standing to my feet and rebuking the man giving the talk. Oh, how I wanted to preach Christ to these people! By halfway through the meeting, the shallowness, the emptiness, the blasphemy of it all had become just too much to bear. The time for my response to God's call had arrived.

I got up from my seat, exited the Kingdom Hall, and began the two-block walk back to my parents' house, where I was living. I started to jog, then to run. It would soon be all over.

I reached the house and went up to my room. Closing the door behind me, and kneeling beside my bed, for the first time in my life, I called upon the name of Jesus (1 Cor 1:2). I repented of my futile, failing life as a servant of the Watchtower. I renounced the Watchtower Society as a blasphemous, man-made counterfeit of Christianity. And, at long last, I accepted Jesus, the *real* Jesus, as my all-sufficient Savior and Lord, and invited Him into my heart.

I was in the truest sense leaving all things to gain Christ (Phil 3:8). I was saying goodbye to everything that was dear to me. The Watchtower theology, to which I had given my all, was now to me less than worthless. The Organization, for so long my sole source of spiritual food, would never again be there for me. Every one of my dear friends, whom I loved with my very soul, would never again be able to speak to me, nor even greet me, but instead only think and speak of me with utter disgust and contempt. Never again would I be able to even carry on a conversation with my brother Steve.

As I prayed I soon became aware that I was lopping off such a huge portion of my life that I might never recover from it. I began to feel that I might not emerge even from that prayer a sane person. But be that as it may, I was willing, even eager to give up also my emotional stability, shaky as it then was, to gain Christ.

I so badly wanted to be through with the whole ordeal that immediately upon rising from my prayer, I began to scribble out a disassociation letter. I still had time to get it down to the Kingdom Hall before everyone left for the night.

But just then there was a knock on my door. It was Brad. I explained to him what was going on, and he sensed the awesome, abysmal despair and chaos that was enveloping me. He felt the pain. So deep.

"It's done," Brad said, trying his best to console me. Then, after a few minutes of further discussion, Brad asked me, "Do you want to pray?" I answered, "Yes."

I was immediately struck with the difference in Brad's prayer compared with that which I had known as a Jehovah's Witness. We bowed our heads, and before beginning to speak, Brad waited in silence for a minute or so. And then as he spoke, I could almost *feel* the vital link that Brad had with his God, his only possible source of strength in this situation. And his prayer was so *personal!* As though his Father was right there in that room with us. After praying, my heart was calmed somewhat.

Steve then arrived home, as he was staying at our house for the weekend. He came up to my room and began accusing and chastising me for not submitting to the Society. He accused me of not fully searching out the Watchtower's explanations on all of the topics in my study. It meant nothing to Steve that I already knew them, having studied them exclusively and intensely for the past seven years. He said that I had not been putting in enough "field service" hours, and therefore Jehovah's spirit had been withdrawn from me. He accused me of "bad association," referring to my association with Brad over the past few months. These accusations Steve continued heaping upon me for an hour or so, adding pain upon pain to my already precarious condition.

But somehow, Steve's accusations weren't quite as devastating as they were intended to be; there was something going on inside of me of which Steve could not be even remotely aware. My strength was no longer my own; my own strength had died with the "old man" who had been crucified earlier that evening. I witnessed for Christ.

A little later Brad and I were alone in the living room. We talked of God's love quietly in the dark. My heart was again comforted.

But sleep that night was fitful. My heart again sank into deep despair. "Who am I? What have I done?" I found myself wondering as I awoke time after time. "What is happening to me?" The battle was still raging! My mind reeled in Scriptural mayhem, verse after verse replaying themselves over and over again in my mind, pitting themselves one against another in endless, senseless anarchy. I felt as though I were desperately clutching at the fringes of reality. But amidst the furor, something else was also happening inside me, and it was something that I'd never experienced before. As I awoke again and again that night, I detected as it were a small, quiet voice inside me repeating spontaneously, "Let God be praised. Let God be praised."

The following day was Saturday, and I was still in shock. Steve continued his reproof.

The next day, Sunday, instead of attending the meeting at the Kingdom Hall, I went for a ride on my motorcycle. Though it was a cool November day, the sun was out, and I needed to get outside for awhile.

After a short ride I found myself at the elementary school that I had attended in fifth and sixth grades. I turned off my bike at the rear of the school, and walked around the playground for awhile. I remembered my childhood there, and I thought of the happy, simple life that I had known then. I sat on the edge of a large sandbox, opened my pocket-sized New Testament, and read through the Book of Galatians. Freedom in Christ! I saw how distressed Paul was that his brethren had been allowing themselves to be held in bondage to other men, and how free and simple genuine Christian life really was. I stood up, put the little New Testament back in my pocket, and looked up to heaven. Romans 8:15 came to my mind: "For you have not received a spirit of slavery leading to fear again, but you have received a spirit of adoption as sons by which we cry out, 'Abba! Father!'" I pulled out my New Testament again and read the next verse: "The Spirit Himself bears witness with our spirit that we are children of God." My eyes flooded with tears. That verse was talking to *me!* The Society had no part in this matter. God Himself was my Father, Jesus Christ, who had taken all my sins upon His own body and died for me (1 Pet 2:24), was my only Lord and Savior (Jude 1:4), and the Holy Spirit had come to dwell with me and *in* me forever (John 14:16-17)! I had been born again!

I got back on my motorcycle and continued my ride. After fifteen minutes or so, I was riding past a building in Clinton Corners with lots of cars in back, and a sign out front caught my eye. "Evangelical Free Church." "Hey," I thought to myself, "isn't that Brad's church?" I had never been there before, and my happening on it by "accident" caught me off guard. Ginny's words rang in my ears, "Since I've come to know the Lord . . ." I pulled over onto the opposite side of the road and studied the building for awhile. I wondered whether there were really demons inside, as the Watchtower had taught us. Or might God have something in store for me there? I saw Brad's motorcycle parked next to the building. "Let God's will be done," I said to myself as I motored back onto the road and headed for home.

8

Disassociation

I met with Larry, the Hyde Park elder who had studied
with me during my summers home from college, together
with his wife Dotti and my brother Steve (at my request),
at Larry's home the following Monday night.

After stating my case before Larry, Dotti, and Steve, the
accusations began afresh. Larry accused me of being "too
much of a philosopher," and said that I had "always been
that way." He also derided me for being "too intelligent."
After realizing that these allegations really meant nothing, he began accusing me of having too much of a desire to
please my Dad! Of course, my Dad had nothing whatsoever
to do with these things. Larry was grasping at straws. Like
Steve, he was incapable of facing the issue head on. As
with all devout Witnesses, he was amazingly incapable of
even allowing the thought into his mind that someone had
honestly determined that the Organization was wrong.

As the evening progressed, and as I continued witnessing, Larry became more and more disturbed, and at times
became very angry. I could see that the foundation of his
life, the Watchtower Society, was being severely shaken.
The foundation of my new life, however, Jesus Christ, was
being demonstrated as unshakeable. I remained wonder-
fully calm during our several hours of discussion, sus-
tained and comforted by the Holy Spirit.

The next Sunday afternoon I met again with Larry, this time at the Kingdom Hall together with Jamie and my brother Steve, for the purpose of giving the elders my letter of disassociation. Steve would not normally have been present at this meeting, but knowing that this would be my last opportunity to witness to him, I had requested that he be there.

For two hours we discussed many of the topics that I had covered in my study, including the deity of Christ, the personality of the Holy Spirit, the return of Christ, and salvation. As I witnessed to them, both Larry and Jamie became more and more upset. They refused to look at my two-inch-thick stack of study notes. When they had finally seen that my new faith in Christ could not be shaken, they asked inquisitively whether I had been born again. When I answered, "Yes!," Jamie retorted scornfully, "So you're going to join the born-agains? Don't you know that they kill one another?" His normally smiling face was red with anger.

Finally, when they had heard enough, Larry asked me, "Kevin, do you have something for us?" "Yes," I answered, and handed him my letter of disassociation:

November 24, 1984   Kevin R. Quick
                           Hyde Park, N.Y. 12538
Jehovah's Witnesses
Crum Elbow Rd.
Hyde Park, N.Y. 12538

Dear Friends,

As you well know, over the years I have had many questions as to the accuracy of various teachings of the Watchtower Society. In an effort to dispel all doubts as to the reliability of this organization's basic doctrines, I have recently undertaken a rather extensive, personal, and objective study of the Bible.

Many hundreds of hours and over seven hundred compiled scriptures later, my clear conscience will no longer

allow me to uphold the convictions common among
Jehovah's Witnesses, and any further identification with
the Watchtower Bible and Tract Society on my part would
only be hypocritical.

Please accept this letter as my voluntary request for disassociation from the organization known as Jehovah's
Witnesses.

Sincerely,
Kevin R. Quick

"So, what are you going to do now?" Larry asked me as
we exited the Kingdom Hall and walked out to the parking
lot. "I'm not sure," I answered, "whatever God leads me to
do. Maybe publish my study notes, possibly write a book
about all that I've been through with Jehovah's Witnesses;
whatever God leads." As we approached Larry's car I
reminded him of what Dotti had told me five years before:
that if she was to ever find out that Jehovah's Witnesses
did not have the truth, she would leave. I challenged him
on this and asked him to give Jesus a chance in his life.

I then walked over to Jamie's car and offered Steve, who
was sitting in the back seat, a copy of my study that I had
made for him. He refused, as I had expected that he would.
As they drove off, heading back to Watchtower Farms in
Wallkill, I called to them my final words: "Let Jehovah be
praised!"

I got into my car and headed home. As I drove up the
street toward my parents' house, Brad's fiancée (now his
wife) Leslie was driving down in the opposite direction. We
stopped for a minute and talked.

"It's done!" I said. "I'm no longer a Jehovah's Witness! I
just gave the elders my letter of disassociation. I'm free!"

Yes, for the first time in seven years, I was free! As Jesus
had said, "If therefore the Son shall make you free, you
shall be free indeed" (John 8:36).

9

Life in Christ

The following Sunday I attended church for the first time. I was terrified! All that I knew at that time about church was what I had learned at the Kingdom Hall, that the churches were infested with demons, and that no true Christian would ever dare set foot in one. But all during my exodus from the Watchtower I had kept a Scripture verse in mind that had given me strength: "But for the cowardly . . . their part will be in the lake that burns with fire and brimstone" (Rev 21:8). As a matter of principle I had determined that as God opened doors before me, I would walk through them come what may.

I walked through the foyer of the Evangelical Free Church in Clinton Corners together with Brad and Leslie. We climbed the stairs to the balcony and were seated there. As the service began, the organist played some soft music, and I relaxed somewhat. Then, Pastor Jon Heymann walked to the front of the platform and asked, "Is there anyone here visiting us for the first time? Would you please stand up and tell us your name and where you're from?" I stood up, a little hesitantly, and answered, "My name is Kevin Quick. I'm from Hyde Park." I heard gasps from the congregation around me and from down below. "It's very good to have you with us today, Kevin." I could tell that Jon was genuinely pleased to have me there that day, and after the service, several people introduced themselves to me and said that they had been praying for me.

I enjoyed the service, and I enjoyed meeting my new brothers and sisters afterwards. My initial fears melted away as I began to understand what true Christian fellowship was all about. Though I had just met them, I really *loved* these people! We were not joined together so much by the knowledge that we carried in our minds, as are Jehovah's Witnesses, but by the personal relationships that we each had in our hearts with Jesus. Like that night after my accepting Christ as Savior, when my heart spontaneously cried out, "Let God be praised!," so now as I fellowshipped with these born-again Christians, my heart was saying as it were, "Amen! Amen! You love Jesus too? Amen!" I knew that I was one of them, and I loved them! We were all one in Christ (Rom 12:5).

After several months of fellowship at the Evangelical Free Church, I was baptized by Pastor Jon "in the name of the Father and the Son and the Holy Spirit" (Matt 28:19).

Life as a Christian and life as a Jehovah's Witness are as different as day and night. The foundation of my new life, my personal relationship with Christ, is a glorious, immovable foundation (Matt 7:24-25). My righteousness is no longer my own; I indeed have no righteousness in myself. But positionally I am, as are all true Christians, "in Christ," inseparably joined to Him forever. His impeccable righteousness has been imputed to me, not by works that I have done, but by the work that He has done for me, which righteousness I have simply received by faith (Eph 2:8-10). And experientially, I can testify that God is at work in me, both to will and to work for His good pleasure (Phil 2:13). As I walk with Him day by day, I experience His sanctifying work in me, from the inside out. I am enabled at all times by the Holy Spirit who indwells me to live a life that is pleasing to my heavenly Father. Many of the old, fleshly desires that I used to be plagued with both before and after becoming a Jehovah's Witness were entirely taken away when I accepted Christ. And of those that still remain, not one of them is any match for the indwelling Holy Spirit as I yield my life to Him.

Since coming to Christ, the Bible is a brand new book for me. Passages that were once dark and mysterious are now glorious, full of light and life. Oh, how joyous to experience the teaching ministry of the Holy Spirit (John 14:24, 1 John 2:27)! I am sometimes moved to tears of joy and thanksgiving when I read of what my Savior has done, how He loves me, and how He is so patiently preparing us to spend eternity with Him.

Bible study has turned from obligatory tedium to one of life's most wonderful adventures. Bible study, whether it be at church, Sunday school, small group gatherings, or alone at home, has proven to be a rich source of spiritual nourishment for me. Unlike Watchtower indoctrination, true Christian studies are boundless. Scholarly works on nearly every subject imaginable are available for objective study. Studies in Christian theology and church history are ready and waiting for the seeker. Christian bookstores are packed with reference Bibles, books, and tapes to instruct the Christian. Before entering a Christian bookstore, I always make it a point to pray to my Father that He might direct me to the materials in the store that I would benefit from most. I've yet to be disappointed!

Weekly church services, so difficult for me that first time, have proven to be a wonderful source of Christian fellowship and edification. My fellowship with other Christians is enjoyed not on the basis of an enforced organizational unity, but on genuine love and concern for one another. Communion services are especially beautiful and touching for me, having been denied this special fellowship with Christ for many years. Regarding doctrinal unity, I have found agreement on the essential doctrines of the Christian faith among all of the dozens of evangelical ("born-again") churches that I have visited over the past several years, together with charitable room for differences of opinion on relatively inconsequential matters. I've found the Watchtower's incessant accusation of profound doctrinal disunity among evangelical churches to be wholly unfounded.

Worship of God is another glorious aspect of Christian life that I was entirely unacquainted with as a Jehovah's Witness. As Witnesses, we *never* worshiped God. We talked a lot about "Jehovah's pure worship," we had meetings, we sang songs, but we never worshiped Jehovah. Now, at Christian meetings, in personal prayer, indeed at all times, I've found worship to be a most natural and enjoyable aspect of my new life. From the first "Let God be praised!" that flowed spontaneously from my heart on the night that I accepted Christ, until this very day, unfeigned worship is the unceasing expression of my new heart toward Him.

Serving God is no longer the tedious chore that it was as a Jehovah's Witness. Rather than obligation, I am motivated now by love; love for God and love for people. As I yield to Him, as His love is shed abroad in my heart, I feel something of the compassion that God has for our lost world; that same love that impelled Jesus to leave His glorious place in heaven to come to earth and die for us. Likewise, I now serve God not because I *have* to, but because I *want* to. And as you might expect, having spent a number of years with Jehovah's Witnesses, I especially have a tender place in my heart for them. Though my efforts to reach out to my former brethren with the love of Christ are often very stressful and emotionally painful for me, still I care for them and do what I can. A few examples will illustrate how I've attempted to reach out to them and how they've responded.

A few weeks after my disassociation from the Organization, as I returned home from church one Sunday afternoon, a group of "Farm brothers" was walking down our street, out in "field service." After a silent prayer to my Father, I walked down the driveway and out to the street, Bible in hand, and proceeded to witness to them. As I spoke to them about Jesus, they acted as though I was not there;

they didn't even acknowledge my presence! It was like witnessing to a stone wall! Still, I was able to at least demonstrate that I had no fear of them, that I indeed loved Jehovah God and His Son Jesus more than ever, and that I really cared about them. "Give Jesus a chance in your life," I said to them finally as we neared the Kingdom Hall at the end of our street. Then I turned back and walked home.

Approximately six months later, again after returning home from church one afternoon, I noticed that the circuit overseer's travel trailer was parked behind the Kingdom Hall. Wishing to demonstrate to my former brethren that I had valid reasons for taking the course that I had, and that I was not "like a wolf, endeavoring to devour Jehovah's weakest sheep in the congregation" as the Society had charged that the "apostates" were accustomed to do, I drove down to the Kingdom Hall. As I pulled into the parking lot, Bob, one of the congregation elders, spotted me and dashed into the Hall. After a prayer, I walked into the Kingdom Hall, a copy of my study in hand. The elders were standing in a tight circle at the back of the hall, talking with the circuit overseer. As I approached, their eyes became fixed on me. "I'd like to talk with the circuit overseer," I said. The circuit overseer spoke up, "What about?" "I assume that you know who I am," I said. "I noticed your trailer out back and thought that I ought to come and talk to you, so you might know exactly who I am, what I've come to believe, and why I'm doing the things that I'm doing." (I had recently begun a recorded message telephone ministry in the area in an effort to reach out to Jehovah's Witnesses.) "I once was where you are," the circuit overseer answered coldly. I offered him the copy of my study that I'd brought for him, but he wouldn't take it. Refusing any further dialogue with me, the elders ushered me out the door.

On a business trip to Colorado, I spent a day in Colorado Springs, and attempted to witness to my friends in Manitou Springs, just a couple of miles away.

I first went to Rex's piano shop. Rex was an elder in the

Foothills congregation whose company I had enjoyed very much. I'd often stop in and visit with him at his shop, and we both delighted in my testing out his pianos once or twice a week. This particular day Rex was not in. Rex's helper, Tracy, a close friend of mine for many years, was on the phone. Tracy saw me, and at first made no acknowledgement of my presence. When he hung up the phone, however, he said, "Kevin, I don't want to hear anything that you have to say. You know what you've done, having left Jehovah and His organization, and I don't want to have anything to do with you. Please leave." I tried to defend myself, "Tracy, I have not left Jehovah. I thought I could at least talk to you for a minute . . ." He cut me off, "If you don't leave immediately, I'm going to have to call someone to get you out of here." So I left the shop, amazed at how effective the Society's smear tactics are in destroying even the closest of friendships.

I then drove to Tony and Karla's apartment. Tony and Karla were also very close friends with whom I had gone on many skiing trips, etc. We had shared many, many intimate times together. I knocked, and Karla came to the door. She was, understandably, very surprised to see me there with a Bible in my hand. "Is Tony here?" I asked. "No, he's not," she answered. "Well," I said, "I guess you could say that I'm out in field service today, and I was hoping that I could talk with you and Tony about the Bible." "I'm afraid we're not interested," she said. She closed the door.

I went to Dean's house and knocked on the door. The screen door was closed, but the main door was open. Looking through the screen, Dean's wife Jean noticed that it was me, and said, "I can't talk to you." "I know that, Jean," I said, "but you and I both know that if it was up to us, you wouldn't be treating me like this. I have something that I'd like to give to you and Dean . . ." As Jean came toward the door, she said, "I think I'd better just . . ." and she closed the door in my face. Before leaving, I put the copy of my study that I had brought for them into the mailbox next to the door.

Back in Hyde Park, I had another opportunity to witness to Larry, the elder with whom I had studied for several years. His wife Dotti, the "pioneer," had been visiting Mary, a close friend of my younger sister Cheryl. When Mary mentioned to Dotti that her friend's brother (me) had left the Witnesses, and thereafter her other brother (Steve) would no longer speak to him, Dotti answered that it was *my* choice to leave "Jehovah's people," not theirs. She gave Mary the impression that I no longer wanted to have anything to do with my friends, Jehovah's Witnesses, and that therefore my ostracism from Steve was by my own choice.

About a week later, again on my way home from church, I saw Larry walking out of the Kingdom Hall toward his car. After a quick prayer, I drove into the Kingdom Hall parking lot, got out of my car, and approached Larry as he was about to get into his car. "Larry," I said, "I need to talk to you about something. Apparently word is being spread around by members of this congregation that I no longer want to have anything to do with my friends, Jehovah's Witnesses. That simply is not true. If you choose not to have anything to do with me, that's entirely *your* decision, not mine. I wish you would make this clear to the congregation." "Kevin," Larry said, his face twitching nervously, "*you* decided to leave Jehovah's organization. It was *your* decision. Nobody forced you to do it. You knew what the bylaws of this organization are; you knew what the consequences would be." "Yes, Larry," I answered, "but that's not the issue. Yes, I chose to leave this organization, but no, it was not and is not my desire to have nothing to do with Jehovah's Witnesses. Now that I've become a Christian, I love Jehovah's Witnesses more than ever!" Still, Larry seemed incapable of separating the two issues. "No, Kevin, it was *your* decision." Anger was rising in his voice as he continued, "You are spreading what we consider to be unclean teachings. It was *your* choice to have nothing to do with Jehovah's people." "Larry," I said as compassionately as I could, "you're an intelligent person. In a very short time I could prove to you beyond a shadow of a doubt that the Watchtower Society is *not* God's organization. It would do not only you but all of Jehovah's Witnesses well to recognize who Jesus is, and to come to Him for salvation . . ." Shaking almost uncontrollably now, Larry said, "Kevin, you've made your decision, and that's that!" He got into his car and closed the door.

I've been unable to witness to my brother Steve. I do see him from time to time. I always say "hi" and try to let him know that I care about him, and that I'd love to talk with him, but he simply turns away coldly and won't have anything to do with me. Brad, however, since he was never a Witness, can and does share with Steve from time to time. And of course, we're both praying for him.

So although seeing and thinking about my Jehovah's Witness friends and my brother Steve is often very painful, I'm not as distressed by it as I could be. I've come to realize that as a Christian I should expect to be persecuted for the cross of Christ (Gal 6:12). And with God's continual enablement through the Holy Spirit, I can indeed obey Jesus' admonition to "love your enemies and pray for those who persecute you" (Matt 5:44). And from the bottom of my heart I can honestly say together with my Lord, "Father forgive them; for they do not know what they are doing" (Luke 23:34).

10

Appeal and Conclusion

The trauma that I experienced during my pilgrimage through the Watchtower is by no means exceptional. The testimonies of countless thousands of ex-Jehovah's Witnesses are considerably more tragic than mine, many culminating in severe emotional instability, depression, hopelessness, and even suicide. The tragedy to me in this appalling state of affairs is that it is all so utterly unnecessary! Now that I've told my story, I'd like to conclude by making an appeal to you, my reader, whether you are studying with Jehovah's Witnesses, an active Jehovah's Witness, or a Christian interested in reaching out to Jehovah's Witnesses.

If you are currently studying with Jehovah's Witnesses, I hope that my experiences will help you to avoid most of the mistakes that I made during my seven years of involvement with them. It's been well said that "The emptiest and unhappiest occupation in the world is trying to act like a Christian when you are not a Christian." You don't need to discover this truth through your own grueling pilgrimage through the Watchtower. First and foremost, I invite you to come to Jesus personally in prayer, asking Him to forgive your sins and inviting Him to come into your life. Trust

Him as your all-sufficient Lord and Savior. Don't let
Jehovah's Witnesses sell you their "good news of Jehovah's
established (since 1914) kingdom." The Bible speaks of
how the apostle Paul "delivered to you as of *first importance* what I also received, that *Christ died for our sins*
according to the Scriptures, and that He was buried, and
that He was raised on the third day according to the
Scriptures" (1 Cor 15:3,4). And Peter likewise says that
"He [Jesus] Himself bore our sins upon His body on the
cross, that we might die to sin and live to righteousness; for
by His wounds you were healed" (1 Pet 2:24). You see, the
real Christian gospel is simply this: Jesus died on the cross
in your place, enduring for you the *full* retribution due
your personal sins; past, present, and future. Accept this
truth, believe it, and you will be born again! Then after
accepting Christ, don't ever allow yourself to be enslaved to
a small group of domineering men as I have. If you ever
detect such a tendency in your own life, read the book of
Galatians to see how Paul dealt with the Judaizers of his
day, and follow his sterling example.

If you don't have a good, understandable, independently
translated Bible (I recommend the New American
Standard Bible or the Revised Standard Version, among
many other good ones), then be sure to get one and read it
regularly. Always preface your reading with prayer to your
heavenly Father in Jesus' name, that He may guide you in
your reading. Be open and attentive to the teaching ministry of the Holy Spirit, your personal Guide in all your
Bible reading and study.

Study Bible doctrine diligently, always with Jesus as the
source and center of your doctrine. Other Christian books
will be of help to you here. You may want to visit your local
Christian bookstore to pick up some good study materials.
If you're not sure where to start, talk with the owner of the
bookstore and get his recommendations. He'll be familiar
with the materials in his store, and he'll undoubtedly be
eager to help you in any way that he can.

As you grow in your knowledge and understanding of

the Bible, have as a goal the continual development and deepening of your personal love relationship with Jesus.

In time, and as God leads you, I encourage you to visit several evangelical ("born-again"), Bible-based churches in your area. You may have some Christian friends that could help you here. When you find a good one (not a perfect one!), get to know some of the people there. Ask them about local Bible study groups; a small-group Bible study is an excellent place for you to learn, share with others, and grow spiritually.

If you are currently one of Jehovah's Witnesses, I would like to offer you some insights that may clear up some mis-apprehensions that you might have about born-again Christians. First of all, born-again Christians don't hate Jehovah; they love Him! Neither do they hate His Name; it is used often in their sermons, books, and hymns. They have simply followed the New Testament pattern of mag-nifying, calling upon, and bowing to the "name above all names," Jesus (Phil 2:9,10)! Also, Christians don't hate you; they love you! At the doors they often refuse to talk with you, not because they hate you, but because they're afraid of you. Just as you may have a fear of greeting and talking with an "apostate," in the same way many Christians are afraid of talking with you, a presenter of a false gospel. They will even quote the same verses that you do when considering your proper conduct toward an "apos-tate," namely, 1 John, verses 9 and 10. And in nearly all cases, though it hurts me to see it happen, it's simply easier for them to close the door than to enter into a meaningful conversation with you. Not knowing enough about you, they are understandably apprehensive.

I must speak frankly with you, my Witness friend, as I know you would with me if our situations were reversed. You must recognize your position before Jehovah; without Christ, you are lost. First John 5:12 is very explicit: "He who has the Son has the life; he who does not have the Son of God does not have the life." Romans 8:9 says, "If anyone does not have the Spirit of Christ, he does not belong to

Him." Notice in verse 15 that this same Spirit is that by
which Christians with the heavenly hope cry out, "Abba!
Father!" If you do not have this Spirit, you do not belong to
Christ. Even more than that, according to God's Word at
Galatians 1:8 and 9, the curse of God abides upon you, a
preacher of "another gospel." But that's not the end of the
story. There is wonderful hope for you. You can be saved
now, and you can *know* that you have eternal life (1 John
5:13). The only condition is that you come to Jesus (John
5:39,40), the *real* Jesus, and trust Him alone for your salvation. I know that this decision won't be easy for you. As
I did, you're going to have to be willing to lose everything
to gain Christ (Phil 3:8). But we have Jesus' own assuring
words, "The one who comes to Me I will certainly not cast
out" (John 6:37).

Your integrity to Jehovah need never be broken. Your
Bible knowledge will not be lost. Much of your knowledge
and your zeal for service will carry over into your new
Christian life.

If you do accept Jesus as your personal Lord and Savior,
and if you do come out of the Watchtower, my dear brother
or sister, I have a couple of recommendations for you. First
and foremost, read, reread, and reread your Bible (a good
translation, of course!). Take it literally whenever there is
no good reason to do otherwise, and don't be afraid to take
it personally. Allow God to lead you into fellowship with
other believers. And don't be afraid of the "apostates."
Many of them, but by no means all of them, have found
Christ in the same way that you have. After I had left the
Organization, I was amazed to find that there were hundreds of ex-Jehovah's Witnesses that had independently
come to the same conclusions that I had, and had also been
born again! You won't be alone. And those ex-Witnesses
that have been born again are nothing like the Watchtower
describes them. I've personally met several hundred of
them, and they are unquestionably some of the happiest,
most loving, most *Christian* people that I've ever met.
Don't fear them. They're the few people on earth who will

be able to fully empathize with you. At the present time local ministries and support groups for Christian ex-Witnesses are springing up all over this country and elsewhere. There are annual conventions of Christian ex-Witnesses in several different locations around the globe. If you can make it, we'd love to see you at the next "Witnesses Now For Jesus" convention held each fall at the Blue Mountain Christian Retreat in New Ringgold, Pennsylvania. An abundance of Christian testimony, teaching, and fellowship awaits you there!

And finally, my brothers and sisters in Christ, I have a few things that I'd like to share with you. If you are like many of the Christians that I've shared with over the past few years, and even if you've read this far in this book, you may still have some misunderstandings about Jehovah's Witnesses that need to be cleared up.

Jehovah's Witnesses are not intentionally rebellious, evil people. It's true, they don't know Christ, but they're not out to trick you. They're *victims* of an authoritarian religious organization, and they need your help. They're hung up on their own "accurate knowledge." They believe that they know infinitely more about the Bible and God's kingdom than you do, and they have very little patience for what they consider to be emotional ignorance on your part. They most likely will not listen carefully to your testimony, though this is often a very good way to witness to them, for fear that the "truth" in their own hearts may be corrupted. Remember the man and woman in Potsdam who prayed for Jim and me and how we reacted to it? Jehovah's Witnesses are not interested in emotionalism. They're interested in the Bible, and they're interested in *substance*. You need to know this. And yet Jehovah's Witnesses are people, too, like you and me, and they too have feelings, so we need to be sensitive. And above all, we need to not just feel sorry for them, but to *love* them and *help* them. But how?

We must prepare for service. Bible study is an absolute must. It is virtually impossible to make progress with a

Jehovah's Witness with only superficial familiarity with God's Word. Sadly to say, at the present time the average Witness knows the Bible far better than the average Christian. Is it any wonder that Christians often get tied into pretzels when discussing Scripture with Jehovah's Witnesses? Happily, though, many Christians and churches are waking up to the rich missionary field that presents itself at their doorstep every few weeks, and are regularly, diligently preparing to "contend earnestly for the faith that was once for all delivered to the saints" (Jude 3). Basic Christian theology and apologetics are at the top of the list of things to be studied in order to be prepared to deal effectively with Jehovah's Witnesses. There are also several good counter-cult ministries throughout the United States that serve as excellent sources of material on all the major cults. I have listed several of them at the back of this book, and I encourage you to get on their mailing lists and to support them prayerfully, and even financially if possible.

Why the need to witness to Jehovah's Witnesses? Consider this. Jehovah's Witnesses will not read Christian literature. They will not read Christian books. They will not attend church, nor will they listen to Christian radio or watch Christian television. There is therefore only one source left by which they might hear the gospel of Christ, believe, and be saved. It's YOU!

But how to witness? There are three basic methods, all of which can be used very effectively.

First, if you know the Bible well, and are familiar with Christian and especially counter-cult apologetics, you may want to take the doctrinal approach. The deity of Christ and salvation are probably the two best subjects that you could discuss with the Witness. Salvation may be the most effective, since the Witness will be ill prepared to defend his position, which is ambiguous at best. Any subject, however, when presented with clarity and skill from the Scriptures, can be effective when witnessing to a Jehovah's Witness.

Second, if you are familiar with the history of the

Watchtower Bible & Tract Society, you may want to take the historical approach. Tactfully, yet firmly, present to the Witness, from his own literature if possible, some of the unfulfilled predictions made by the Society over its past hundred-year history. Ask the Witness about the invisible presence of Christ since the year 1874, or about the end of the world in 1914, 1918, 1925, 1942, and 1975. Ask him about the earthly resurrection of Abraham, Isaac, and Jacob in the year 1925, and about Beth Sarim, the palatial mansion built for them by "Judge" Rutherford in San Diego. Couple these predictions with the Watchtower's own claim to be God's end-time prophet, His sole channel of communication with mankind. Ask him to read Deuteronomy chapter 18, verses 20 through 23, which explains how we are to respond to a "prophet" who speaks in Jehovah's name but whose predictions fail to come true. Ask him about the Society's history of doctrinal change; about the Society's past and present views of vaccinations, organ transplants, and the "superior authorities" of Romans chapter 13. Skillfully using the historical method, you can begin to drive a wedge of apprehension between the Witness and the organization that has so cunningly deceived him.

Third, whether you know the Bible well or not, and whether you are familiar with Watchtower history or not, if you are a Christian you can always use the devotional approach. Share your personal testimony with the Witness. Tell him what Jesus means to you, and how He has changed your life. Speak to him of your personal relationship with Jesus. You'll be planting some seeds deep in his heart that, with God's gracious care, will grow to fruition in due time.

A couple of final points about witnessing to Jehovah's Witnesses. Do your best to remain on one subject at a time. This may be difficult, as the Witness will likely jump from subject to subject whenever he feels cornered. Something that many have found to be effective is to agree beforehand with the Witness that you'll not deviate from a certain subject until you've fully made your point. Then, when he attempts to jump to another subject, write down his objection, promising to discuss it a little later, and return to the subject at hand. Then, after fully making your original point, finish up by answering his objections that you have written down.

A final point that I'd like to stress is that whether or not you make any genuine progress with the Witness, he's not going to show it. His loyalty to the Organization will force him to put up a front of impenetrability. So don't necessarily expect any immediate, demonstrable results from your witnessing efforts. But don't despair; by God's grace seeds are being planted. Remember, it took seven years of witnessing by at least twelve different Christians before I finally came to Christ.

As this book draws to a close, I'd like to conclude by thanking my God, my blessed Father in heaven, for a few things that have become very dear to me.

I thank my Father for His written Word, which proved to be an unfailing light to me, even in the darkest hours of my search for Him. I thank him for the Christians who took the time and effort to speak to me about Jesus when I didn't yet know Him. I thank Him for His glorious salvation, which I have been enabled to receive only by His grace. I thank Him for my new brothers and sisters in Christ, "the church of the living God, the pillar and support of the truth" (1 Ti 3:15). I thank Him for the blessed hope of the church, and for the coming full manifestation of His kingdom, in which all things in heaven and on earth will praise and glorify Him perfectly, for all eternity. And finally, and above all else, I thank Him for Jesus, my precious Lord and my only Savior, who has made all of these things possible.

For further help please contact:

Comments from the Friends
P.O. Box 840
Stoughton, MA 02072

Kevin Quick
P.O. Box 123
Staatsburg, NY 12580

Watchman Fellowship
P.O. Box 7681
Columbus, GA 31904

Personal Freedom Outreach
P.O. Box 26062
Saint Louis, MO 63136

Bethel Ministries
P.O. Box 3818
Manhattan Beach, CA 90266

Endnotes

1. The circuit overseer is a traveling representative of the Watchtower Society who visits each of the congregations in his "circuit" every four months or so. One of his primary functions is to ensure that each of the congregations is following the organizational policies laid down by the headquarters staff in Brooklyn.

2. Reasoning from the Scriptures, p. 277

3. Former "Bethel family" member Bill Cetnar writes in his book, *Questions for Jehovah's Witnesses,* "From my observation, N.H. Knorr, born 4/23/1905, baptized 1922, Cedar Point OH, and died 6/5/1977 age 72; F.W. Franz, 4th President born 1893, Albert D. Schroeder, G.D. Gangas, and M. Henschel met together in these translation sessions. Aside from vice-president Franz (and his training was limited), none of the committee members had adequate schooling or background to function as critical Bible translators. Franz's ability to do a scholarly job of translating Hebrew is open to serious question since he never formally studied Hebrew. This came out in the Scottish Court of Sessions in November 1954.

4. Reasoning from the Scriptures, p. 150

5. Ibid., pp. 136-137, 282-283; Aid to Bible Understanding, p. 919

6. Reasoning from the Scriptures, pp. 136-137; Make Sure of All Things, p. 487

7. Ibid.

8. Reasoning from the Scriptures, pp. 424-425; Watchtower, 9/1/68, p. 583

9. Reasoning from the Scriptures, p. 209, pp. 282-283

10. Aid to Bible Understanding, p. 1329

11. Ibid.

12. Reasoning from the Scriptures, pp. 282-283

13. Aid to Bible Understanding, p. 1329

14. Ibid., p. 1533

15. Reasoning from the Scriptures, pp. 101, 375

16. Ibid., pp. 136-137, 382
17. Ibid., p. 383
18. Ibid.
19. Ibid., p. 382
20. Ibid., p. 333
21. Ibid., p. 334
22. Ibid., p. 333
23. Ibid.
24. Make Sure of All Things, pp. 229-242
25. Reasoning from the Scriptures, p. 103; Make Sure of All Things, p. 231
26. Make Sure of All Things, p. 146
27. Watchtower, 11/1/68, p. 649
28. Reasoning from the Scriptures, p. 225
29. Ibid., p. 224
30. Reasoning from the Scriptures, p. 268
31. Aid to Bible Understanding, p. 683
32. Life Everlasting in Freedom of the Sons of God, p. 161; Our Incoming World Government-God's Kingdom, p. 120
33. Reasoning from the Scriptures, p. 137; Make Sure of All Things, p. 303
34. Reasoning from the Scriptures, p. 166
35. Watchtower, 1/15/69, p. 51
36. Life Everlasting in Freedom of the Sons of God, pp. 185-186
37. Ibid.
38. Watchtower, 6/15/68, p. 359
39. Watchtower, 10/1/67
40. Life Everlasting in Freedom of the Sons of God, p. 364
41. Watchtower, 1/1/86, p. 23
42. Watchtower, 12/1/68, pp. 733-735
43. Reasoning from the Scriptures, p. 356
44. Ibid., p. 52
45. Ibid., p. 53
46. Watchtower, 8/15/34, p. 249
47. Watchtower, 9/1/54, p. 529; Watchtower, 10/1/67, p. 587; Watchtower, 12/1/81, p. 27
48. Watchtower, 11/15/81, p. 21
49. Watchtower 5/1/81, p. 17
50. The Truth that Leads to Eternal Life, pp. 23, 121
51. Watchtower, 11/1/68, pp. 652-656
52. Watchtower, 12/1/68, pp. 733-735
53. Watchtower, 2/15/86, pp. 12-14
54. Ibid., pp. 14, 20
55. Reasoning from the Scriptures, p. 360
56. Ibid.

57. Ibid., p. 358

58. Watchtower 6/15/68, p. 359

59. Watchtower 12/1/85, p. 9

60. Aid to Bible Understanding, p. 1386

61. The Truth that Leads to Eternal Life, p. 182

62. Aid to Bible Understanding, p. 1388

63. Watchtower 6/15/68, p. 359

64. Ibid.

65. Watchtower 12/1/85, p. 18

66. Ibid.

67. Ibid., p. 7

68. Aid to Bible Understanding, p. 1329

69. Reasoning from the Scriptures, pp. 268, 324-325; Watchtower, 2/15/86, p. 15

70. Watchtower, 2/15/86, p. 15

71. Reasoning from the Scriptures, pp. 95-97

72. Ibid.

73. Watchtower, 2/16/85, p. 16

74. Reasoning from the Scriptures, pp. 314, 343; Make Sure of All Things, p. 451

75. Babylon the Great has Fallen, p. 458

76. Ibid.

77. Aid to Bible Understanding, pp. 551, 1336

78. Reasoning from the Scriptures, p. 137

79. Watchtower, 12/1/85, p. 17

80. Ibid., pp. 17-18

81. Ibid.

82. Reasoning from the Scriptures, p. 436; Make Sure of All Things, p. 166

83. Ibid.

84. The Watchtower is evidently quite proud of this fact. In a recent Watchtower book, *Revelation—Its Grand Climax at Hand!,* on page 36 is found this statement: "In the songbook produced by Jehovah's people in 1905, there were twice as many songs praising Jesus as there were songs praising Jehovah God. . . . But in the latest songbook of 1984, Jehovah is honored by four times as many songs as is Jesus."

85. The complete study, which I've self-published and entitled *Reasoning with Jehovah's Witnesses,* is available from the ministries listed at the back of this book.